# The Future of the Past

EDITED BY
JANE FAWCETT

NIKOLAUS PEVSNER

NIKOLAUS BOULTING

JOHN BETJEMAN

OSBERT LANCASTER

JANE FAWCETT

MARK GIROUARD

ROBIN WINKS

HUGH CASSON

THAMES AND HUDSON
LONDON

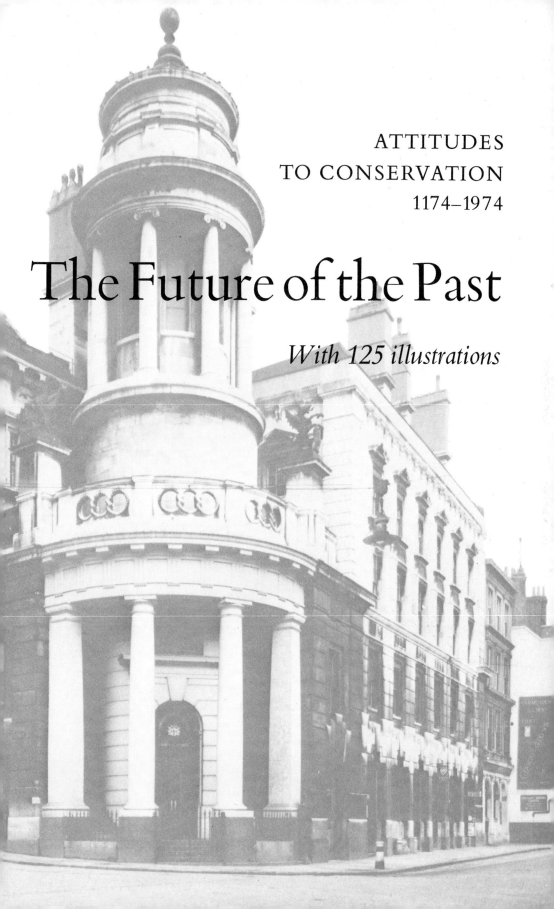

ATTITUDES
TO CONSERVATION
1174–1974

# The Future of the Past

*With 125 illustrations*

Printed and bound in England by
Cox & Wyman Ltd, London, Fakenham
and Reading

# Contents

*The rage of repairing . . . will be little less fatal
to our magnificent edifices
than the Reformation and the Civil Wars.*

THOMAS GRAY to James Bentham, probably written in March 1765,
on Bentham's *History and Antiquities of the Conventual and Cathedral
Church of Ely*

## Photographic acknowledgments

(*Numbers refer to pages*)
Aerofilms 22; Birmingham Post and Mail 29; British Museum 77, 95;
Civic Trust 26; Gerald Cobb 98; Country Life 54, 63, 116, 120–123,
125, 126, 129, 130, 133–135, 137, 139; Courtauld Institute 76, 77;
Department of the Environment, Crown copyright 21; J. R. Freeman
41; Guildhall Library 89; A. F. Kersting 20, 93; Sir Osbert Lancaster
64, 73 (from *Temporary Diversions* (left) and *Recorded Live* (right),
published by John Murray), 73; National Monuments Record 10, 11,
16–19, 21–25, 27, 28, 31–34, 45, 61, 74, 79, 82, 85, 88, 89, 95, 98, 101,
107–109, 111, 127; Library of Congress, Washington 140; Mrs
Pouncey 16; J. E. Rackham Ltd 86, 87, 104; Rev. M. Ridgway 82,
93; Dean and Chapter of Rochester 79; Royal Commission on
Historical Monuments, Crown copyright 41; Royal Institute of
British Architects 96; Science Museum 60; Society of Antiquaries 83,
107; The Times 23; United States Department of the Interior 147,
149; United States Information Service 148; Victoria and Albert
Museum 108.

# Introduction

THE title 'The Future of the Past' was coined by Sir Osbert Lancaster for an essay which was first published in the Journal of the Royal Institute of British Architects in 1953 and we are grateful to Sir Osbert and to the RIBA for permission to reprint it.

I used the phrase in 1970 as the title of a lecture which, as Secretary of the Victorian Society, I was invited to give at the Smithsonian Institution in Washington. The theme of the lecture, as of this book, was the changing attitudes towards historic buildings from the Reformation to the present day. I concentrated largely, but not exclusively, on British examples and tried to trace a gradually developing conscience and a growing sense of responsibility towards their care and protection.

This theme inspired an exhibition, promoted by the Victorian Society and arranged by Nikolaus Boulting and myself, with the same title, which was first shown in London at the Central School of Art and Design in 1971. Nikolaus Boulting's illustrated account of a slowly evolving protective legislation, from 1174 to the present day, is drawn from this source. The exhibition was later acquired by the Victoria and Albert Museum. Two versions of it have since travelled around Britain and are still available from the Museum's Circulation Department.

At the time of this exhibition the Victorian Society also arranged a series of accompanying lectures. Three of them, by Sir John Betjeman, Professor Robin Winks and Sir Hugh Casson, have been adapted and expanded for the present book. The contributions by Sir Nikolaus Pevsner, Dr Mark Girouard and myself were specially written and appear here for the first time.

The Victorian Society, formed in 1958, has been largely responsible for developing aesthetic criteria for the art and architecture of a hitherto much neglected and often derided period. The Statutory List of Buildings of Architectural and Historic Importance was compiled in close cooperation with the Society and it is now regularly consulted by the Government and by local authorities on architectural problems and on threats to important Victorian and Edwardian buildings. Even so, the losses continue and the threats remain.

Much has been written during the past fifteen years – some of it inspired by the Victorian Society – extolling the virtues of Victorian architects. Here we have attempted to redress the balance by documenting some of the ineptitudes of these architects and the pitfalls into which their over-confidence led them. Both Sir Nikolaus Pevsner and I have re-examined some of the problems faced by leading Victorian architects when dealing with buildings of an earlier period, and our papers are closely linked. Dr Girouard, having previously established the qualities and the social backgrounds of Victorian patrons of architecture, here examines their attitudes to existing country houses. Sir John Betjeman remembers the sources of his architectural inspiration and influences which led him, and he us, to an interest in Victorian buildings, and he retreads his own footsteps in his inimitable way. Sir Osbert Lancaster's reflections on replicas, restoration and the reconstruction of classical sites have lost none of their relevance. Professor Winks, formerly United States Cultural Attaché in London and now Professor of History at Yale University, stresses the historical bias of American conservation, the sites of important battles or significant birthplaces, even if redeveloped, taking precedence over architectural considerations. Finally Sir Hugh Casson, as well known for his architecture as for his brief pioneer book on Victorian buildings; he can teach us that modern architecture and a passion for Victorian architecture can happily exist together.

However, this is a rarity. One of the ironies of architectural training is that it has been based on the study of old buildings, but has seldom bred a respect for them. Given a choice between conservation or replacement, most architects have chosen to rebuild. Since this book is devoted to the care of historic buildings, it seemed an appropriate context in which to make a re-assessment of the successes and failures of the past.

The book could not have been compiled without the help of many members of the Victorian Society. In particular I am indebted to Sir Nikolaus Pevsner and Alec Clifton-Taylor for their kindness in making corrections to the text of my paper. I would also like to thank the Society of Antiquaries, the Society for the Protection of Ancient Buildings and many cathedral archivists; and in addition Stephen Dykes-Bower, Judith Nucci, David-William Torrington, Phillis Rogers, Sophia Ryde and Helena Clarke for their help in different ways.

JANE FAWCETT

# I  The law's delays: conservationist legislation in the British Isles

## NIKOLAUS BOULTING

### Introduction

TODAY we are acutely conscious of the need to preserve relics of the past, and buildings which are thought historically or architecturally interesting may be given a degree of legislative protection. This concern, however, is in no way peculiar to the twentieth century, or even to modern times. In the Dark Ages, a building's prestige was determined by its historical associations. The scene of St Alban's martyrdom in 301, for example, was thought to be endowed with miraculous powers of healing and consequently, when Christianity was re-established in Britain, provided the ideal site for a church. Bede tells us that the wooden buttress of a church on Farne Island against which the dying St Aidan leant in 651 was not only endowed with healing properties but was also apparently fire resistant, and was incorporated in successive buildings on that site before being preserved as a relic of the Saint. On his arrival in Kent in 598 St Augustine found the remains of two Romano–British churches, St Martin's to the east of Canterbury and the foundation he rededicated to Christ, now of course the cathedral. Repaired and enlarged, these churches linked the new Christian mission with the earlier Romano–British Christian world. Here, and in numerous other instances which Bede recounts,[1] we see the significance of historical association. How-ever, the preservationist attitude even for devotional reasons was the exception to the rule. The Anglo–Saxons and the Norman invaders, who had little respect for the primitive native architecture, found Roman remains useful quarries, while existing churches often merely marked convenient consecrated sites for their new, larger, more fashion-able edifices. When, then, did people start to become concerned about the preservation of antiquities?

*Canterbury Cathedral, the east end, showing William of Sens's remodelling of the older choir*

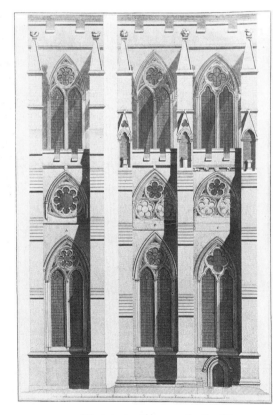

*Westminster Abbey, north side of the nave, showing the meeting of thirteenth-century work (left) and Yevele's matching continuation of the late fourteenth (right)*

## Emotional ties – 1174

Architects competing for the commission to rebuild the cathedral church of Canterbury, after the fire of 1174, were, as Gervase intimates[2] and as the building itself shows, required to preserve as much as possible of the original fabric of Conrad's 'Glorious Choir'. The extent to which Guillaume de Sens and his successor, William the Englishman, actually stuck to the intention of the brief is irrelevant; the important point is that this was typical medieval conservatism, rather than conservationism, born of sentiment rather than any historical concern about monuments of the recent past.

## Sensitivity to the past – 1375

The Middle Ages showed little awareness of the styles of the past: fashion was not in any way dominated by historicism. It is all the more remarkable, therefore, that when, in 1375, Henry Yevele was confronted by the task of completing the thirteenth-century nave of Westminster Abbey, he decided 'to show his reverence for the thirteenth century by continuing with a minimum of change'[3] in the design. In other words, he, or Abbot Litlyngton, was conscious of the importance of uniformity and was not ashamed of building in a style which, by the middle of the fourteenth century, had certainly become unfashionable. Yevele was aware not only of the historical importance of Henry III's coronation church, but also of its architectural significance. Here, certainly, there is evidence of an archaeological awareness of an historic monument. Flying in the face of the wind, he showed a definite sensitivity towards the past, and anticipated the 'dimension of historic time'[4] which the Renaissance was to give to Western culture in the fifteenth century.

## The catastrophe of the sixteenth century

'Archaeology,' wrote Joan Evans, 'like fire-weed, grows best on ravaged land. So long as the fabric of medieval England remained united men were barely conscious of nostalgia for the past. . . . The dissolution of the monasteries between 1535 and 1539 arrested the stream of English life by an unparalleled catastrophe.'[5] The political motives which led to the Reformation of the English Church, and the enormous financial benefits which prompted the impoverished Henry VIII to dissolve so many of the 850 monastic houses then active, also unintentionally led to interest in monuments of the past. Here again we are confronted by the unpredictable consequences of vandalism. Even before the iconoclastic purges of the Dissolution got under way, John Leland, the King's librarian, began to pass favourable comments not only about the manuscripts that he was saving for the Royal Library, but even on the buildings in which he found them: for example, of Saresbyri, or Salisbury, he noted 'The tourre of stone, and the high pyramis of stone on it, it is a noble and memorable peace of work.'[6]

### 'Agaynst breakyng or defacing of Monumentes' – 1560

Interest in medieval buildings as historic monuments was fostered by the Catholic revival of Mary's reign, and culminated in an Elizabethan proclamation of 1560 forbidding the 'defacing of Monuments of antiquity, being set up in the churches or other public places for memory, and not for superstition', instructing offenders 'to provide that no such barbarous disorder be hereafter used, and to repair as much of the said Monuments as conveniently may be'.[7]

*Rievaulx Abbey, Yorkshire, abandoned at the time of the Reformation*

*Part of Queen Elizabeth's proclamation of 1560 'agaynst breakyng or defacing of Monumentes'*

## Awakening interest – 1620

The survey of Stonehenge by Inigo Jones,[8] commissioned by James I in 1620, reflects the awakening of interest in prehistoric and Roman monuments as well as medieval remains. The rather startling conclusion of the survey, that the stone circle was of Roman origin, shows how primitive archaeology was in the seventeenth century. Nevertheless, the profuse topographical and historical studies of the Stuart period, often illustrated by engravings, provide a unique record of the threatened and fast disappearing past.

*Stonehenge, from the 1675 edition of Inigo Jones's survey*

*Inigo Jones's west portico to Old St Paul's Cathedral*

## Correcting the past – 1630

Threats to ancient buildings came from neglect; from natural disasters, like the Great Fire; and from fashionable alterations to buildings, like Inigo Jones's classical portico at the west end of Old St Paul's. Dugdale tells of the 'lamentable condition' of Old St Paul's,

being made a horse-quarter for soldiers during the whole time of the late Usurpation; the stately Portico, with beautiful Corinthian pillars, being converted into shops for the seamstresses, and other trades, with lofts and stairs ascending thereto: for the fitting whereof to that purpose those stately pillars were shamefully hewed and defaced for the support of timber work.[9]

## 'Relicts of idolatory' – 1641

The Commonwealth also brought a deliberate programme of destruction. In 1641 the House of Commons underwrote these acts of vandalism by ordering 'Commissions to be sent into all Countries, for the Defacing, Demolition, and quite taking away of all Images, Altars or Tables turned Altarwise, Crucifixes, superstitious Pictures, Monuments, and Relicts of idolatory, out of all Churches and Chapels'.[10] By these iconoclastic purges Catholicism was ritually exorcized, but, as in the period of the Dissolution, antiquarian interest expanded.

*Cartoon showing different attitudes to iconoclasm in the seventeenth century*

## The eighteenth-century dilemma: preservation – 1721

One surprising threat to the survival of ancient monuments and buildings in the eighteenth century came from the ever increasing demands of traffic. In 1721 the Secretary of the Society of Antiquaries presented 'a bill for Ten Shillings which he [had] paid by order of the Society for setting down two oak-posts to secure Waltham Cross from injury by Carriages'.[11]

*Waltham Cross in the eighteenth century, showing the two oak posts provided for its protection in 1721*

The High Cross of Bristol in situ *next to the cathedral. Later in the eighteenth century it was re-erected at Stourhead*

The
GROANS

Of the Abbeys, Cathedrals, Palaces, and other antient buildings of North Britain.
Illustrious Society. Can you tamely look on, and suffer our bodies
To be basely torn, barbarously mangled, and layed in ruins by a selfish race
of
unfeeling Goths.
Can you tamely look on, we say, and not punish these rude offenders?
Many of us are entirely levelled!
Some of us falling down with gothic groans!
Some of us tumbling down with decay!
Pity our forlorn situation, and procure us the necessary aid, by an
Act of Parliament.
Or soon, too soon alas! None of us will be left to
Groan!

*An appeal 'from the Abbeys, Cathedrals, Palaces and other ancient buildings' to the Society of Antiquaries, 1776*

## The eighteenth-century dilemma: 'progress' – 1733

But the preservationist attitude of the Society was by no means universally held. The citizens of Bristol, in 1733, argued that

> It hath been insinuated by some that this Cross, on account of its antiquity, ought to be lookt upon as something sacred. But when we consider that we are Protestants, and that Popery ought effectually to be guarded against in this nation, we make this our request to you to consider. If the opening of a passage to the four principal streets in this city ought not to outweigh anything that can be said for keeping up a ruinous and superstitious Relick, which is at present a public nuisance.[12]

The subsequent fate of this 'superstitious Relick', the High Cross, reflects a significant change of attitude, for the monument was not simply knocked down, but was dismantled to reappear later in the century in a picturesque setting at Stourhead, when medieval remains were at a premium.

## The Society of Antiquaries of London

From 'about 1585 . . . a number of persons in and about London, eminent for learning, had regular meetings for the improvement and illustration of the history and antiquity of England'.[13] By the time the successors of this pioneer group received their Charter, in 1751, it was clear that they realized their obligation to protect ancient monuments, if possible, as well as record them. Moreover, a letter of 1776 shows that the Society was publicly regarded as the custodian of ancient monuments. The letter shows both public concern for medieval remains and the realization that pressure groups might prove effective in the battle to preserve some of these remains.[14]

## The Antiquaries versus James Wyatt – 1780

By the end of the eighteenth century it became clear that the survival of medieval buildings was threatened as much by the way in which they were restored as by their total destruction. James Wyatt, 'fam'd for knocking down our ancient buildings',[15] restored Salisbury and Durham cathedrals with 'startling thoroughness'[16] between 1780 and 1800. His work at Durham, in particular, provoked an outcry from the Society of Antiquaries. The extent of the restoration, including the rebuilding of the east front and the demolition of the Norman chapter house, was revealed by the drawings done for the Society by John Carter. This first preservation battle was at least partially successful, for Wyatt's design was not completed: the Galilee chapel survived, and the crossing tower was not capped by the intended octagonal tower and spire.

*Drawings by John Carter showing Durham Cathedral before and after Wyatt's restoration, 1780–1800*

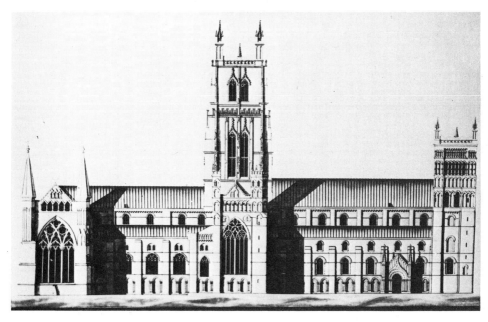

## The Society for the Protection of Ancient Buildings – 1877

Restorations, like that of Durham
Cathedral, threatened the survival of
many medieval buildings during the
nineteenth century. The mantle of
Carter was assumed first by Pugin and
then by Ruskin, and it was their
passionate interest in medieval
architecture, and especially their concern
about the deceit of restoration, which
provoked Morris into forming the
Society for the Protection of Ancient
Buildings when the threat of Sir
Gilbert Scott's attentions being focused
on Tewkesbury Abbey was reported.
Originally founded mainly to protect
medieval buildings, the Society soon
turned its attentions to those of other
periods. Between 1884 and 1896 seven
of Wren's City churches disappeared:
but as early as 1879, the SPAB had been
instrumental in saving St Mary-at-Hill.
Morris emphasized the historical
arguments for preservation.

> It has been most truly said . . . that
> these old buildings do not belong to us
> only; that they have belonged to our
> forefathers and they will belong to our
> descendants unless we play them false.
> They are not in any sense our
> property, to do as we like with. We
> are only trustees for those who come
> after us.[17]

Morris argued, echoing one of Ruskin's
themes from the 'Lamp of Memory':

> I must not leave the truth unstated,
> that it is no question of expediency or
> feeling whether we shall preserve the
> buildings of past times or not. *We
> have no right whatever to touch them.*
> They are not ours. They belong
> partly to those who built them, and
> partly to all generations of mankind
> who are to follow us.[18]

*Choir of Tewkesbury Abbey before and after
Sir George Gilbert Scott's restoration of
1877*

## The Ancient Monuments Protection Act – 1882

In 1875 the Austro–Hungarian ambassador wrote to Lord Derby, the Foreign Secretary, to ask what was done to protect ancient monuments in the British Isles. Lord Derby found his answer in a letter from the Society of Antiquaries, in which the Society 'deeply regrets that no legislative machinery is in this country available for the conservation of monuments of the character specified . . . [and their] protests are too often sterile in their results, because they are unable to summon to their aid the strong arm of the law'.[19] From 1873, Sir John Lubbock had introduced various Bills in the House of Commons for the protection of ancient monuments; all were opposed for the same reason, that they appeared to involve unjust interference with private property. However, in 1882, Lubbock's Bill finally became law.[20] The Ancient Monuments Protection Act (1882)[21] was a compromise. Its principal provision was that the Commissioners of the Board of Public Works could, with the owner's consent, take into guardianship, or acquire, and maintain at public expense, any monument included in a short-list. This short-list, or 'schedule', listed sixty-eight monuments in the British Isles, all but a few of which were of prehistoric origin — earthworks, burial mounds and stone circles.

## 'They are ruins . . .' – 1889

The Act offered protection to monuments that were for all practical purposes useless, and were therefore least likely to be restored, and were hardly likely to be removed at whim. Moreover, the Act specifically excluded from its protection all ecclesiastical buildings that were in use. Although the Act made vandalism by members of the public punishable, by fine or imprisonment, the owner of an ancient monument was still at liberty to destroy or neglect his property. Nothing in the Act compelled the owners to hand over the guardianship of monuments to the Commissioners, or to ensure their upkeep. In 1889 the Commissioners informed the owner of the ruins of Glastonbury that his property was in a bad state of repair. His answer, which perfectly summarizes the faults in this first piece of protective legislation, was simple: 'Well, they are ruins now, and if they fall they will be ruins still, won't they? What more do you want?'[22]

*Ruins of Glastonbury Abbey, before 1889*

*The Clergy House, Alfriston*

## The National Trust

Realizing the threat of industrialism to the countryside and the ancient buildings of England, Octavia Hill, Sir Robert Hunter and Canon Rawnsley founded the National Trust. The Trust was empowered to acquire, and preserve for the nation, places of historic interest and natural beauty, and the National Trust Act of 1907[23] ensured that property left to, or acquired by, the Trust could not be sold or radically altered. The foundation of the Trust was the logical sequel to the formation, in 1865, of the Commons Preservation Society and, in 1877, of the Society for the Protection of Ancient Buildings, and represents the fulfilment of Ruskin's dream that an association should be formed, with a fund, to protect buildings and land, if need be by the acquisition of freeholds. Since its earliest acquisition in 1895, Dinas Oleu, four and a half acres overlooking the Barmouth Estuary in North Wales, the Trust has acquired over 400,000 acres, and is, apart from the government and the Forestry Commission, the largest landowner in the country. The first building the Trust took into its custody was a medieval timber-framed building, the Clergy House at Alfriston. Today the Trust owns over two hundred houses which are open to the public, in addition to many other properties, like the farmhouses and buildings on its estates.

*Richmond Castle, Yorkshire, protected under the Act of 1900*

## The Ancient Monuments Protection Act – 1900

The Ancient Monuments Protection Act of 1900 offered protection to medieval buildings as well as to prehistoric remains. If the Commissioners thought that the preservation of a monument was necessary and desirable because of its 'historical, traditional or artistic interest',[24] they or the local authority could, with the consent of the owner, assume guardianship. Again the Act specifically excluded ecclesiastical property, and, curiously, any occupied property.

## The Ancient Monuments Consolidation and Amendment Act – 1913

In 1911 Tattershall Castle was destined to be dismantled and at least part of it shipped to the United States. This new threat to our historic buildings forced people to realize the need to extend the very limited powers of the previous Acts. The Ancient Monuments Consolidation and Amendment Act (1913)[25] made two significant contributions to protective legislation. First, the Commissioners were empowered to publish lists of monuments whose preservation was considered, by the Advisory Historic Monuments Board, to be of national importance. Second, an element of compulsion was introduced: the owner of a scheduled, that is a listed, monument was notified that he was obliged to apply for permission to alter or demolish his property. If a scheduled monument was threatened by destruction or damage from injudicious treatment or neglect, then the Commissioners were empowered to make a preservation order, placing the monument under their protection. The 1913 Act, therefore, both listed important monuments and provided legal means for ensuring their protection, by enabling either the local authority or the Ministry of Works to assume guardianship or to acquire ancient monuments, and to maintain them at public expense. It also redefined the punishments for injuring or defacing ancient monuments: a fine, not exceeding £5, and the cost of repair, or a term of imprisonment, with or without hard labour, not exceeding one month.

## The Act tested – 1914

The Act was first put to the test in 1914, when a preservation order was placed on 75 Dean Street, Soho, one of a block of four early Georgian houses, distinguished by a painted staircase –

*Tattershall Castle, Lincolnshire*

*Detail from the staircase of 75 Dean Street, London*

wrongly attributed to both Sir James Thornhill and to his son-in-law, William Hogarth – and by some finely decorated rooms. Despite the fact that he had spent a considerable sum on the restoration of this house, the owner could no longer afford its upkeep. Much to the horror of both *The Times* and

*Country Life*, whose comments reflect the way in which public opinion was already beginning to turn in favour of preservation, a court·ruled that the 1913 Act did not allow for adequate compensation to be paid to the owners of buildings subject to preservation orders. After World War I, 75 Dean Street suffered exactly that fate which the 1913 Act was intended to avoid: it was dismantled and the staircase was shipped to the States, where it was reconstructed in the Art Institute, Chicago.[26]

*Interior of Wren's All Hallows', Lombard Street, demolished in 1936*

## The position of the Church – 1913 and after

'I would be the last to deny that on occasions in the past ecclesiastical property has not always been protected as it ought to have been, but the utmost care is taken now to prevent a repetition of anything of the kind.'[27] With these words Archbishop Davidson, in 1913, offered reassurance to those, including the SPAB, who were worried that ecclesiastical buildings were not protected by ancient monuments legislation. How did this anomalous position arise? Was it, as Lubbock suggested in 1882, that the restorations of the nineteenth century showed that there was no agreement over methods of preserving medieval churches? Was the Church, still a formidable political force in the country, jealous of interference by the State? Or was the State wary of becoming financially liable for the upkeep of so many buildings of historic significance? Diocesan Advisory Committees were set up to advise on alterations and repairs to churches: by 1923 they had been appointed in thirty-one of the thirty-eight dioceses. In spite of the existence of these watchdogs, however, it was only pressure from the City Corporation, the LCC and the SPAB which defeated the Bishop of London's attempt to demolish no fewer than nineteen City churches, in 1926: his intention was to divert their incomes into the parishes of outer London. Ten years later, the destruction of Wren's All Hallows', Lombard Street, showed the inadequacy of the system, and the futility of those reassurances given in 1913.

## The Ancient Monuments Act – 1931

*Hadrian's Wall, near Housesteads*

The Ancient Monuments Act of 1931[28] authorized local authorities to set up preservation schemes to protect not only monuments but also the areas surrounding them. The need for this legislation was shown, for example, by the quarrying being carried out under and around Hadrian's Wall. This legislation, which was designed to protect ancient monuments by strict planning control in the immediate environs of a monument, introduced the concept of the conservation area into protective legislation.

## The Town and Country Planning Act – 1932

At the discretion of the local authorities, preservation schemes could be set up to protect buildings, or groups of buildings, other than ancient monuments. Within such a scheme, the demolition of a building of architectural or historic interest could be avoided if the local authority chose to impose a building preservation order. Ironically, there were no lists of buildings which were thought worthy of preservation to guide the authorities: consequently, the owners of significant buildings were not obliged to inform local authorities of their intention to demolish.[29] In 1927 the Norwich authority anticipated the Act, when, on the advice of the SPAB, Elm Hill was earmarked for conservation, and purchased.

*Elm Hill, Norwich*

*Bath from the air*

*Adelphi Terrace, London, demolished in 1937*

## The City of Bath Act – 1937

In Bath frequent use was made of the building preservation order, and, no doubt inspired by the legislation of 1932, the Bath Corporation Act was passed in 1937 to help to preserve the character of the city as the threats to this unique piece of eighteenth-century town planning increased.[30]

## The Georgian Group – 1937

'It must be remembered that the period between the wars was that of Jacobean cocktail bars and spurious Knole sofas, when Georgian buildings were dismissed as dull square boxes.'[31] Today no one questions the need to preserve Georgian buildings, but in the 1930s those 'dull, square boxes' were constantly being threatened. Rennie's Waterloo Bridge was destroyed in 1932; the west side of London's Bedford Square was to have been demolished for a new road scheme; and Brighton's Royal Pavilion was condemned, by the Brighton Corporation, as a hideous and useless white elephant. The destruction of Adam's Adelphi Terrace, in 1937, provoked the formation of the Georgian Group, a preservation society concerned with buildings dating from 1714 to the 1830s. It was soon evident that the passionate polemics of Pugin and Morris were not always the most effective way of fighting preservation battles: Nancy Mitford threatened to chain herself naked to the railings of the House of Commons if Abingdon Street, Westminster, was demolished. The street, and the public, were spared – though the street was irreparably damaged during World War II.

## World War II – 1939–45

The widespread destruction of buildings by aerial bombardment in 1940 brought the plight of historic buildings to the attention of the public and Parliament. In 1941, the National Buildings Record, which is now incorporated in the National Monuments Record, the first systematic photographic record of English architecture, was founded: it was inspired by the desperate need to record those fast disappearing 'monuments of our art and history'. Obviously nothing could be done to protect historic buildings from the holocaust of war, but the dramatic loss of buildings at this time emphasized the need for legislation to make historic buildings less vulnerable to other threats.

## The Town and Country Planning Acts – 1944 and 1947

The Town and Country Planning Acts of 1944[32] and 1947[33] introduced comprehensive lists of buildings which were thought worthy of preservation because of their architectural or historic interest. When a building was listed by the Ministry the local planning authority and the owner and occupier were informed; the onus was then on the owner to notify the authority of his intention to demolish or make radical alterations to his listed property. If the authority objected to the proposed demolition or alteration, they could then impose a building preservation order, leaving the owner, of course, with the right to appeal to the Minister. The

*Wilton House, Wiltshire, a building 'of such importance that its destruction should in no case be allowed'*

*The Iron Bridge, Coalbrookdale, 'a landmark of the Industrial Revolution'*

*The Pagoda, Kew, an architectural 'freak'*

instructions to the Ministry's Investigators shows the complexity of drawing up lists of buildings of special interest. 'In Grade I will be placed buildings of such importance that their destruction should in no case be allowed. . . . In Grade II place those buildings whose preservation should be regarded as a matter of national interest', and whose demolition should not be allowed without compelling reason.

Grades I and II formed the statutory list: but the Investigators were also asked to make supplementary lists of 'buildings which have a cumulative group value, but which do not have that degree of intrinsic architectural or historic interest that would naturally be called special'.[34] The owners of buildings on these supplementary lists were not informed, and were therefore at complete liberty to demolish their property without reference to their local planning authority. The criteria by which buildings have to be assessed are equally complicated. A building may be a 'work

of art, the product of a distinct and creative mind'; or it may typify a school of design. It may present a fascinating combination of architectural styles, or it may be an architectural 'freak', and worth preserving for its rarity value. Again, the instructions state clearly that engineering is a significant part of the history of architectural design: 'certain industrial buildings are landmarks of the Mechanical and Industrial Revolution, and thus certainly ought to be listed.' Finally, the Investigators were advised on the proportional quantity of buildings that should be listed. Almost all buildings dating from before 1725 which have survived in more or less their original form, and the majority of those which date from before 1800, should be listed. For buildings erected after 1800 the degree of selectivity should become more and more stringent, so that late nineteenth- and early twentieth-century buildings were very seldom offered protection under this original system of listing.

## Historic Buildings and Ancient Monuments Act – 1953

In past times, the great houses of this country and their grounds were maintained by their owners mainly from the rents of their estates. The estate and the mansion formed a single economic whole; the former provided not only income and produce but also servants to run the house and craftsmen for the upkeep of the fabric. Now, owing to economic and social changes, we are faced with a catastrophe comparable only to that which the country suffered by the Dissolution of the Monasteries in the sixteenth century.[35]

The Gowers Committee, which was concerned with the question of how these great country houses were to be preserved, recommended that the owners of outstanding houses should be eligible for tax relief and relief from death duties to offset the enormous cost of maintenance. This idea has never found its way into the statute book, but prompted by other suggestions and the threat of catastrophe the Historic Buildings and Ancient Monuments Act of 1953[36] enabled the Minister, on the advice of the Historic Buildings Councils, to make grants for the repair and maintenance of buildings of outstanding interest, and their contents. It also enabled the Minister to acquire, or help local authorities to acquire, these buildings.

The Local Authorities (Historic Buildings) Act of 1962[37] made more money available for the upkeep of interesting buildings, irrespective of whether they are listed, and including for the first time, churches in ecclesiastical use. The significance of the inclusion of churches is obvious: but the fact that Councils have the discretion to make awards towards the upkeep of unlisted buildings of local rather than national interest is often overlooked.

*The decay of the country house: Blatherwycke Park, Northamptonshire, in 1911 and 1948. It was demolished a few months later*

## The Civic Trust

Progress in urban and rural planning may mean two things: the initiation of new schemes, or the redevelopment of historic areas, adapting existing streets, zones or towns to the changing demands of the present day. In 1957 Duncan Sandys founded the Civic Trust to encourage a greater awareness of the problems of town planning on the part of both the local planning departments and private developers.

The Town and Country Planning Act of 1932 advised local authorities to protect historic areas by initiating preservation schemes: but the legislation was more 'exhortation than teeth'.[38] Certainly the significance of the group value of the Georgian terraces of Bath or Cheltenham was realized and measures were taken to preserve them; but little had been done to protect the gradual erosion of streets and town centres of historic interest.

## The Victorian Society – 1958

By the 1950s it was accepted that Georgian architecture was worth the inconvenience of preservation: but little was done to protect Victorian buildings, as the Ministry lists were biased towards buildings dating from before 1800. 'No one listens to what we say, and "Oh, it's only Victorian" means that it can be ruthlessly destroyed,'[39] Lord Esher complained at the first Annual General Meeting of the Victorian Society in 1959. Though unsuccessful, the campaigns to preserve the Euston Arch and the London Coal Exchange both created an interest in Victorian architecture and emphasized its vulnerability. In retrospect, those campaigns illustrate perfectly the lack of imagination and the ruthlessness of the planner. The Doric Arch, as a monument to the Age of Steam, would have provided the necessary focal point in that empty

*The decay of townscape: Chippenham High Street in about 1900, 1934 and 1955*

*The Euston Arch, demolished 1962*

piazza in front of the new Euston
Station. As for the demolition of the
Coal Exchange in 1963: the road-
widening programme which necessitated
the immediate removal of this important
early industrial building has still to be
carried out. These, and numerous similar
test cases, certainly helped to focus the
traditional blind eye that was turned
towards threatened Victorian buildings:
while the outcry engendered by the
recent battle to save government
buildings in Whitehall from destruction
itself demonstrates how far opinion on
the merits of Victorian architecture has
changed since 1959.

*A designated Conservation Area: the city of Cheltenham, showing on the right one of the environmental disasters which the scheme is designed to prevent in the future*

### Civic Amenities Act – 1967

The philosophy of the conservation area, fostered by the Civic Trust, was the kernel of a private Member's Bill which Duncan Sandys steered through Parliament in 1967. The Act instructed local authorities to make and constantly revise a list of areas of architectural and historic interest which were to be designated as conservation areas.[40] While the character and appearance of these areas were to be preserved and enhanced by strict planning control, the Act made no provision for the protection of buildings, other than listed buildings, within such a scheme; offered little in the way of advice on the problems of reconciling the economic and social developments of the twentieth century with the preservation of our old towns; and gave no significant financial incentive to make the idea of conservation attractive to the local authorities on whose good will it relies.

Important advances were contained in the Town and Country Amenities Act of 1974.[41] Previously, even if a building was sited in an area which had been designated for conservation, unless that building was listed its owner was free to demolish it without the permission of the local planning authority. Now the demolition, or radical alteration, of all buildings within conservation areas, excluding sheds and walls, etc., must be sanctioned by the planning authority.

The historical accident which placed the property of churches of all denominations outside the protection offered by the ancient monuments and all subsequent historic buildings legislation, also threatened the survival of buildings other than churches. In 1964, a court ruled that 6 Gower Street, the rectory of St George's, Bloomsbury, was, legally speaking, an ecclesiastical building in ecclesiastical use. This ruling endangered rectories and deaneries, church schools and many other buildings, like those in our famous cathedral closes. The Civic Amenities Act cleared up this anomaly. Parsonages, and other buildings which though owned by a church are not themselves church buildings, have been brought within normal historic buildings planning control.

## The Town and Country Planning Act – 1968

The Town and Country Planning Act of 1968[42] increased the degree of protection which the Acts of 1944 and 1947 had offered to listed buildings. It provided legal means of dissuading those bent on destroying or neglecting historic buildings by the threat of punishment; and it introduced spot listing, which, in speeding up the cumbersome mechanics of listing, extends protection to numerous threatened buildings. The Act also increased the degree of responsibility of the local authorities in sanctioning the demolition of historic buildings; it gave specialist preservation groups and local amenity groups a consultative role; and it helped the Royal Commission on Historic Monuments to develop its archive of buildings past and present. Under the provisions of the 1944 Act the onus had been on the owner of a listed building to inform the local authority of his intention to demolish; many owners failed to give the necessary notice, and their failure meant that there was no early warning system to alert the local authority, or Ministry, or amenity groups.

*Sill Hill Hall, Solihull, a seventeenth-century timber-frame building, demolished by the owners, without consent in 1966*

### Punishments

In 1966, Sill Hill Hall, Solihull, which under the Town and Country Planning Act of 1947 was listed, and ought to have received protection, as a Grade II historic building, was demolished without reference to the local planning authority. Under the law, at that time, the maximum punishment that could be imposed for such vandalous acts was a fine of £100 – the teeth had been extracted from the ancient monuments legislation of 1913 which had threatened imprisonment with hard labour! However, the punishments for offences against the Town and Country Planning Act of 1968 were intended to act as real deterrents: the same offence committed today could result in an unlimited fine or imprisonment for not more than one year.

*Neglect*

Furthermore, neglect and deliberate neglect are actively discouraged under this piece of legislation: local authorities are empowered to compulsorily purchase any listed building which is suffering from neglect, after warning the owner of their concern, at a price which excludes the value of the site for redevelopment.

*Spot listing*

In order to protect buildings of special interest which have not already been listed, the local authorities or the Department of the Environment may serve emergency building preservation orders, which, within a matter of hours, offer these buildings full statutory protection. This protection is effective for six months, after which the Minister must decide whether the buildings concerned should be added to the statutory list. Since the introduction of these powers, over two thousand buildings have been saved by spot listing, the vast majority of these being nineteenth- and early twentieth-century buildings which had previously been neglected as a result of the extreme selectivity advocated in the original instructions to the ministerial Investigators.

*Listed building consent*

Another positive step which the 1968 Act took was the introduction of listed building consent. The local planning authorities must now actively sanction the intended demolition of, or any alterations to, a listed building, by giving listed building consent.

*Consultation*

At the same time, local authorities are obliged to notify the various amenity societies concerned, including the SPAB, the Georgian Group and the Victorian Society.

*Recording*

The Act is also important from the archivist's point of view; as early as the eighteenth century antiquarians had realized the need to record monuments and buildings of past ages by drawing and engraving them. This idea, which was implicit in the work of Stukeley, Carter and other antiquarians, and was made explicit in Ruskin's suggestions to the Society of Antiquaries in 1854, was given legislative backing in 1908 by the establishment of the Royal Commission on Historic Monuments, a systematic archive of important buildings and monuments. Under the 1968 Act, the Royal Commission is informed when listed building consent has been granted, so that they may make a photographic record, if they think that the building concerned is sufficiently interesting.

## Crown and Church

The Town and Country Planning Act of 1968 offered protection to some historic buildings, while specifically withholding it from others. Ancient monuments are, of course, covered by other legislation, but neither Crown buildings nor ecclesiastical buildings in use are subject to special protection.

The number of Crown buildings of architectural or historic interest includes the Royal Palaces and the property of the Crown Estates Commissioners:

government offices, and properties like the official residences of Ministers; the property of government departments, like the War Office, and, of course, the nationalized industries. None of these, as government property, is fully protected by historic buildings legislation. How can this anomaly be justified?

The exclusion of churches from the provisions of both ancient monuments and historic buildings legislation is closely tied up with financial problems:

£2 million are needed for the restoration of York Minster, £3 million to 'save St Paul's': these sums are greatly in excess of the amount which the Department of the Environment spends annually on the upkeep of its numerous monuments and buildings.

Churches may be threatened by demolition because they are redundant, or because they do not meet present-day requirements; and numerous alterations are carried out in the name of liturgical reform. At Salisbury, in 1960, Scott's choir screen was taken down, without reference to the Cathedral's Advisory Committee, a body set up in 1949 to advise on alterations to cathedrals. The Catholic Church has vigorously resisted the idea of outside interference; and as there was no advisory body, disasters – like the loss of the screen from Pugin's St Chad's Cathedral, Birmingham – were inevitable. The loss of this screen was partly vitiated by its installation at Holy Trinity, Reading; Scott's screen was less fortunate, ending up in the breaker's yard.

## Redundant Churches

Now that fewer people are active churchgoers, many churches have, or are destined to, become redundant. The extent of the threat of redundancy is alarming: in 1960 it was estimated that 370 churches were redundant and some 420 were destined to become so before 1980. As many as half of these buildings, it was thought, are of considerable architectural and historic interest.

The Pastoral Measure (1968)[43] set up an advisory board for redundant churches, to advise the Church Commissioners on the architectural and historic value of churches threatened with redundancy. If a suitable alternative use cannot be found for a church which the Board thinks worthy of preservation, the Redundant Churches Fund or the Department of the Environment can take it into custody, at public expense.

*Screen of St Chad's Cathedral, Birmingham, in situ; now in Holy Trinity, Reading*

*St Thomas, Winchester, a redundant Victorian church converted into a library*

*Londonderry House, Park Lane, London*

*Heveningham Hall, Suffolk*

*The Grange, Hampshire; some parts, including the portico, are to be preserved as a ruin*

### Battle honours – (a) outbidden

Successive pieces of ancient monuments and historic buildings legislation have been undermined by one obvious fault: the inadequacy of the funds available to compensate the owners of historic buildings. In 1962 Londonderry House, which was overshadowed by the London Hilton, was sold for redevelopment for half a million pounds. The LCC was understandably reluctant to impose a building preservation order, fearing that they would be called upon to purchase the building, and local government funds certainly do not allow for the sort of expenditure that the acquisition of buildings of this quality, often on highly desirable sites, would involve.

### Battle honours – (b) ransomed

Indeed, it is only in cases of extreme importance that the central government will step in with financial assistance, as it did, when in 1969, Heveningham Hall was sold to the nation for half a million pounds. But this was the fortunate exception to the rule: think of the plight of the Grange, Wilkin's Neo-classical masterpiece. Why did Hampshire County Council, or the Department of the Environment, fail to take steps to ensure its preservation? After all, it was listed in 1956, and was at that time known to be in a delapidated state. Successive pieces of historic buildings legislation have made more money available, both from central and local government funds, for the restoration of important buildings.

### Battle honours – (c) defeated

The 1968 Act contained provisions specifically intended to penalize those who neglect listed buildings. Legally, steps could have been taken to avoid the loss of the Grange, but the effectiveness of the law depends on the ability of the authorities to show their determination to preserve historic buildings by purchasing them out of public funds. The inadequacy of the funds available for compensation or compulsory purchase is the Achilles' heel of protective legislation: without financial backing the legislation which has evolved over the last century can only slow down the speed of destruction, rather than ensure the preservation, of our historic buildings.

## The Economics of Preservation

The economic pressures which militate against preservation are now more powerful than at any time: Poseidon-like freaks of the Stock Market apart, land and property represent the soundest and most lucrative of investments, particularly in the hands of the developer. It is to the developer, therefore, whether in the public or private sector, that the preservationists should pitch their arguments: not simply by being critical, abusively or constructively, but by showing that intelligent cooperation can yield high dividends, financially and aesthetically. Here again, the onus is on the preservationist to convince the developer that preservation is very often more lucrative than wholesale development. There are obvious cases which prove the point: Park Crescent and Nash's terraces around London's Regent's Park, for example; but the economics of preservation have been grossly neglected, and it is figures rather than feelings which will sway the balance, will condemn or ensure a future for the past.

*Nash's Sussex Place, before and after conversion into a residential college*

# NIKOLAUS PEVSNER

*Christchurch, Oxford, the hall staircase, c. 1640*

# II  Scrape and Anti-scrape

HOWARD COLVIN, in a by now famous paper in the *Architectural Review*,[1] tried to distinguish in one area of England between Gothic Survival and Gothic Revival. The problems of restoration which concern us here can be called either. By restoring you pretend to create a survival which does not really exist, but you endeavour to revive what by additions or neglect had been concealed.

The problem arose for the first time on a substantial scale after the Civil War. At Lichfield Cathedral, for instance, in the choir clerestory all but two windows were destroyed or seriously damaged, and in the 1660s Bishop Hackett restored them. He did that without hesitation in their original Perpendicular form and accurately enough to deceive the casual visitor. That this was possible is due to the fact that in church work other than restoration Gothic was still practised by the masons and no doubt expected by the patrons, without as a rule any awareness of a choice. What Inigo Jones had done at St Paul's, the Queen's Chapel in St James's and St Paul's, Covent Garden, and what John Webb considered on paper, remained an exception.

I have scrutinized a volume of my *Buildings of England* which deals with two peripheric counties: Cumberland and Westmoreland. Holme Cultram Abbey (*c.* 1605) received a Perpendicular east window,[2] Arthuret, begun in 1609, looks completely Perpendicular, even though the original east window has tracery details which give away the real date of the church.[3] Survival also is the Perpendicular of Greystoke of *c.* 1645 and of Witherslack of *c.* 1669.

But how about the familiar posthumous Gothic of Oxford? Lord Clark, in his earliest book, was convinced that this also was Survival. I was never able to believe that. Surely the heads of colleges knew what the Court and the nobility and gentry round the Court did. Surely the hall staircase of Christchurch does not appear as it does, because some master mason did not know better. The Gothic of Wadham Chapel is amazingly correct; so are the many lierne vaults and fan vaults, right down to that of University College's Radcliffe Quad of *c.* 1715–19. In fact the case for Revival in the Universities can be proved. I am referring to a document which I have quoted in detail more than once before. The document refers to the library of St John's College in Cambridge.[4] This was built in 1624, and its windows – but only the windows – are so completely Gothic and so unusually correct that I mistook them at first for a Victorian alteration. But they are original, and the scholar who tried to convince the donor of the money of their rightness told him that 'men of judgement liked the best the old fashion of church windows holding it the most meet for such a building'. There is the Victorian attitude complete, the attitude of using Gothic forms for certain tasks as associationally or evocatively most suitable. It is in total contrast to both Lichfield and Cumberland, where Gothic was used naively – as it were, 'before the fall'.

Later in the same century, Wren used different, but equally Victorian, arguments. In 1681 he wrote this to Dr Fell, Dean of Christchurch in Oxford, about the completion of Tom Tower: 'I resolved it ought to be Gothic to agree with the Founder's Work' – i.e. Cardinal Wolsey's – because, and here I am quoting from Wren's Memorandum of 1713 on the completion of Westminster Abbey, 'to deviate from the old form would be to run into a disagreeable mixture which no person of good taste could relish'. So that is Gothic for reasons of conformity. But Wren added a remarkable passage hinting at another reason. He writes that he was compelled to use Gothic occasionally also for parish churches in the City of London, and he calls the result 'not ungraceful but ornamental' – Gothic not for conformity but for its own aesthetic qualities – even if we and our Victorian ancestors might use different attributes by which to characterize the Gothic style.

And in the same year as this memorandum of Wren's, Sir John Vanbrugh used yet a different argument in defence of a medieval building. He pleaded in 1709 that the ruin of Woodstock Manor on the Blenheim estate should be preserved, and his arguments are 'their magnificence and Curious Workmanship' and over and above that the 'lively and pleasing reactions' which they move 'on the Persons who have inhabited them, or the remarkable things which have been transacted in them, or the extraordinary occasions of erecting them'.[5] That, I need hardly say, is the romantic after the aesthetic and the conformist arguments.

The first two can be followed through the eighteenth century, especially in Horace Walpole's letters from the 1740s to the 80s. But during these decades a new attitude appears, and one which at last takes us into our subject proper.

Horace Walpole was a friend and admirer of James Essex, the Cambridge architect. Walpole had a great respect for Essex's knowledge of English medieval architecture and more than once expressed his hope that Essex would write a history of Gothic architecture. This never came about, though plenty of preliminary papers are preserved in the British Museum. But Essex was called upon to add certain furnishings to Ely

Cathedral and Lincoln Cathedral, the former from 1757, the latter from 1761. The work, in the style of the late thirteenth to early fourteenth centuries, is stylistically so accurate that it can easily be mistaken for the real article. This is so, in spite of the fact that Essex also did much re-facing in Cambridge colleges in the Georgian classical style which was standard at the time.

But Essex, in his knowledge of, and respect for, Gothic architecture, was an exception. When cathedral restorations became more urgent and hence more frequent, the most favoured architect, James Wyatt, had neither Essex's knowledge nor his respect.

With Wyatt, Act Two of the drama which I am trying to re-tell opens. The *dramatis personae* from the 1780s to Wyatt's death in 1813 are Wyatt, of course; John Carter, and also the Rev. John Milner. Wyatt was born in 1746, Carter in 1748, Milner in 1752. Milner was a Catholic and an antiquarian of high standing – his history of Winchester, published in 1798–1803, and his *Ecclesiastical Architecture in England*, published in 1811, can be used even now with profit. Carter from 1780 was draughts-man for the Society of Antiquaries, and he also worked for Richard Gough, who was Director of the Society of Antiquaries from 1771 to 1787 and is famous for his *Sepulchral Monuments*, which began to appear in 1786.[6]

James Wyatt's first cathedral restoration was Lichfield, where he started in 1788. This was followed by Hereford, also from 1788, Salisbury from 1789, Durham from 1791. Wyatt, who could handle classical elements and motifs so elegantly, as Heaton Hall and the Radcliffe Observatory prove, had certainly also a vision of medieval grandeur and the sweep forward and upward of Gothic piers, arches and vaults, as his Fonthill proves; but his vision unfortunately was not that of the Gothic masons. For one thing Wyatt believed in the unimpeded through-view from west to east, as the majority of the visitors to cathedrals still do. Now the medieval patrons did not, nor did the Victorian. So Wyatt removed screens and other obstacles. He also proved a thorough Georgian in his admiration for symmetry and uniformity. Thus at Salisbury he moved funerary monuments to places between the nave piers so that they should be neatly in order.[7] And for unity's sake he removed the two porches, north and south, and the Perpendicular chantry chapels of the Hungerford and Beauchamp families which were in a structurally bad state. At Hereford he shortened the nave, gave it a new gallery and put up a new west front which was, however, replaced by the present one in 1908,[8] and at Durham he demolished the east end of the chapter house and replaced the Perpen-dicular central window of the east transept by an Early English rose window of his own invention. It is true that he also intended to pull down the Galilee, the elegantly Late Norman chapel west of the west front, but this was, it seems, less the wish of Wyatt than of the Dean and Chapter, who were anxious to gain a drive up to the west façade.[9]

The *Gentleman's Magazine* was not at first anti-Wyatt. In 1790 a contributor signing Indoctus calls him 'our modern Palladio',[10] in 1793 (Peregrine le Moyne) 'the ingenious Mr Wyatt whose . . . skill and judgement in regard to Gothic architecture are truly . . . unequalled'.[11] Yet opposition against Wyatt's treatment of the cathedral had by then started. R.G., i.e. Gough, accused Wyatt for what he had done at Salisbury. The term improvement should not be used, 'a big sounding word, and often mischievous'.[12] One year later, one Indoctior answers Indoctus more specifically, blaming Wyatt for pulling down at Salisbury 'what he decrees defect in uniformity'.[13] At Hereford, the west tower collapsed in 1788. The reaction of the *Gentleman's Magazine* to Wyatt's restoration was fiercer: 'Such is the rage for renewing this ancient structure, that it seems doubtful, if the whole may be able to resist the experiments intended to be practised on it.'[14] To use the north transept – indeed the most beautiful part of the Cathedral – in place of the former parish church of St John is 'an act of folly and want of taste'.[15] In the same year as this last remark Viator writes about Lichfield: 'The periods of Gothic architecture are cruelly confused, the monuments . . . removed', and ugly buttresses were built to secure the south transept.[16]

Carter mounted the stage in 1795, when he exhibited his unfinished sketches of Durham Cathedral to the Society of Antiquaries which had commissioned them. His remarks on the occasion were true and provocative:

The East Front of the Chapel of the nine Altars . . . is receiving a new Appearance. The gigantic Statues of the Founders and Patrons having been thrown to the Ground, lie confounded with the Fragments of this once august Front. The pavement is to be raised on a level with that of the Church, which will obliterate the whole extraordinary and splendid Range of the Nine Altars. The Choir will change its very Situation, as the Altar Table will be placed against the East Window of the Nine Altars, where, with but few Decorations, it will be dark and obscure. The Seats of the Bishop and the Dean are to be changed from their original Destination – the Stalls, the Feretory of St Cuthbert, the Altar Screen and Bishop Hatfield's Tomb are to be destroyed . . . To regret the devastation continually making in our Cathedrals and other sumptuous Buildings connected with them, will in itself be of no avail, unless some Efforts of laudable and animated Zeal be made for the preservation of the remaining ones, in fact the Royal and Munificent Patron of this Society should be implored to stay in time this innovating Rage and prevent interested persons from effacing the still remaining unaltered Traits of our Ancient Magnificence which are but faintly to be imitated and perhaps never to be equalled.[17]

That was outspoken enough, and it may strike one as odd that after this Wyatt proposed himself for fellowship of the Society of Antiquaries. There was indeed violent opposition, led, it seems, by Milner. Milner on this occasion announced that he wanted to read a paper to the Society entitled 'Dissertation of the modern style of altering antient Cathedrals'.

However, he was not allowed to read it; for Wyatt had influential friends. Although in a first ballot he was black-balled, he was in a second, in December 1797, accepted. So Milner published his paper, linking it up explicitly with the *affaire* Wyatt and the views of those who declared themselves 'incapable of reconciling a zeal for the study of Antiquity with the practice of ravaging the choicest subjects of it'.[18] The building discussed by Milner was Salisbury, and *à propos* Salisbury Milner attacked Wyatt's ideal, 'to reduce each cathedral to a single room' which the buildings 'obstinately resist'.[19] Hence for instance the Beauchamp Chapel, 'the most exquisite model of the style in which it was built', had to go.[20] In his final summing-up[21] Milner speaks of 'devastation' and of 'destructive caprice and false taste', and reinforces his argument by quoting a letter from Horace Walpole to Gough with words like 'barbarous', 'scandalous' and 'dishonest'. The 'Dissertation' came out in 1798. In the same year Milner wrote yet more savagely to the *Gentleman's Magazine*:[22] Wyatt 'has dishonoured, disfigured, destroyed, and is in the constant practice of dishonouring, disfiguring, and destroying . . . the most beautiful and instructive monuments'. It was in the same year that Carter began to write for the *Gentleman's Magazine*. He signed himself 'An Architect' and called his contributions · at first for a while 'The Pursuit of Architectural Innovation'. Carter was an experienced medievalist and a passionate hater of the 'heathenish' style which 'turned the genius of Englishmen from their national architecture',[23] and which in its additions to the Palace of Westminster, he calls 'vulgar' and 'contemptible'.[24] Wren is included in Carter's censures.[25] Carter published several books on medieval architecture and sculpture,[26] and according to Briggs wrote, in the *Gentleman's Magazine* between 1795 and his death in 1817, 212 articles. Here are some quotations from the early ones: *à propos* Peterborough: 'the rage of architectural innovation . . . has spread its devastating and disgusting hand',[27] and *à propos* St Margaret next to Westminster Abbey:[28] 'From what ancient or modern building, either in Rome, France, Egypt, China, Lapland or elsewhere are the peculiar parts selected, or is the style of the whole purely the production of uncontrolled fancy?' The examples could be increased ten and twentyfold. But the quotations given are enough, and so we can end Act Two.

★   ★   ★

Act Three got into its stride only slowly. Meanwhile, as far as design in the Gothic style goes, the demand suddenly grew enormously. Government had become perturbed by the lack of churches in the fast-growing towns of the industrial north, in the likewise fast-growing suburbs of London and in other developing areas. An Act was passed in Parliament in 1818 allocating £1 million to church building. A few years later another half million was granted. The first grant paid nearly wholly for the new churches, the second as a rule only for 10 per cent or less. The intention was to build as many churches as possible as cheaply as possible. The majority of the building was Gothic, because that cost less than Grecian. But they are mostly Gothic only in so far as they have lancet windows and thin and useless buttresses. There are exceptions such as churches designed by Rickman, by Goodwin, by Hardwick. But mostly the Commissioners' churches have a starved look. It represents not only the Commission's attitude but also that of the parochial clergy. Already in 1798 Carter[29] had complained of churches being 'unaired, covered with dust and rubbish' and monuments being 'defiled, mutilated, and used for the most ignoble purposes'. The complaint was true. Canon J. S. Leatherbarrow, in his excellent *Victorian Period Piece*,[30] quotes cases in the 1820s where Holy Communion only took place three times a year, where the recipient of the cup said: 'Here is your good health, Sir,' which was corrected by the next recipient to: 'Here is the good health of our Lord Jesus Christ,' where the parson at baptism instead of using holy water spat into his hand, where the squire had the luncheon tray brought into the family pew when the sermon started, and where the parson during a service climbed on the altar to open a window.

The war to restore to churches ritual and at the same time architectural dignity was waged by one man and one society, the man being a fervent convert to Catholicism, the society calling itself Catholic too, but meaning what is called Anglo-Catholic. They operated independently, but appreciated one another. The man was Augustus Welby Northmore Pugin (1812–52),[31] the society the Cambridge Camden Society.[32] Pugin began to write and fight in 1835, and his most important books came out in 1841 and 1843; the Cambridge Camden Society was founded in 1839 by the Cambridge undergraduates, John Mason Neale and Benjamin Webb, and its journal, the *Ecclesiologist*, started to appear in 1841. Pugin's writings were highly successful, though in some quarters his success was a *succès de scandale*; the same was true of the Cambridge Camden's programme, known as Ecclesiology. Pugin and the Camdenians together created the High Victorian attitude to church buildings – High Church buildings – and that implied church restoration.

Pugin on Wyatt is as good as Carter and Milner on Wyatt. 'All that is vile, cunning and rascally is included in the term Wyatt.'[33] Pugin on church building, however, is new: 'We can never successfully deviate one tittle from the spirit and principles of pointed architecture. We must rest content to follow, not to lead.'[34] But the Catholic architecture of the ages before the Reformation which was to be followed might have been Early Christian, Romanesque (i.e. in England, Norman), Early English with lancet windows, the style of Westminster Abbey, Decorated, or Perpendicular. Commissioners' churches were usually lancet style or, if elaborate, Perpendicular. Pugin from 1839 or 1840 onwards regarded as the climax of English church architecture the style of Westminster

*Church of the Holy Sepulchre, Cambridge, before and after restoration by Salvin in 1841*

Abbey, that is what he called Second Pointed or Middle Pointed. The Ecclesiologists concurred.

Pugin and the Ecclesiologists were also agreed on certain ritual requirements: a sufficiently long chancel for the altar and a surpliced choir, the isolation of chancel from nave by a screen, i.e. of priest from congregation, and more generally on dignity and sacramentality. In Pugin's writings restoration appears only marginally; Neale and Webb not only dedicated space to it in the *Ecclesiologist*, but went themselves into the promotion of restoration. It was they who induced Salvin to restore the Round Church, i.e. the Norman Church of the Holy Sepulchre, in Cambridge. The way the restoration was done gives a foretaste of their attitude. The Perpendicular ambulatory windows were replaced by Norman windows and the bell-turret was removed and a conical roof built instead. This procedure followed the declared principle of the Camdenians. In the *Ecclesiologist* of 1842 we can read: 'To restore is to revive the original appearance . . . lost by decay, accident or ill-judged alteration.'[35] And the principle was applied with zest; for as Neale said: 'How can I but feel the most devoted affection to so noble a cause as that of church restoration?'[36] Already, in the first volumes of the *Ecclesiologist*, the Camdenian principle was set out in unambiguous detail:

We must, whether from existing evidences or from supposition, recover the original scheme of the edifice as conceived by the first builder, or as begun by him and developed by his immediate successors; or, on the other hand, must retain the additions or alterations of subsequent ages, repairing them when needing it, or even carrying out perhaps more fully the idea which dictated them. . . . For our own part we decidedly choose the former; always however remembering that it is of great importance to take into account the age and purity of the later work, the occasion for its addition, its adaptation to its users, and its intrinsic advantages of convenience.[37]

There are ominous turns of phrase in this: 'carrying out more fully', 'taking into account the purity of later work', 'intrinsic advantages of convenience'. The first may mean making a church more Second Pointed than ever it had been, the second the removal of Perpendicular additions, the third the alteration of internal fixtures for the sake of Victorian worship. Indeed a little later the *Ecclesiologist* says: 'We have no hesitation in urging the propriety of entirely removing late super-added clerestories, and restoring the roofs to the form they undoubtedly had when the earlier arcades of the nave were built'[38] and expressed the hope that in a particular case the architect 'will not hesitate to replace the existing late Middle Pointed tracery of the east window with a design of an earlier character, so as to restore it to the state in which it must have been originally erected'.[39]

Support came to the Cambridge group from Oxford. In 1846, E. A. Freeman, later the author of the famous *History of the Norman Conquest* (1867–76), published a pamphlet called *Principles of Church Restoration*. He contrasted the medieval method, which was to continue a building in the style of their own time with a method of today that is not to destroy any medieval work. New work thus in the medieval centuries was in a genuine style, new work now is an imitative style. But there are more problems involved in imitation today. How is one to follow the medieval work? The building to be restored may have parts in several styles. Freeman says that, if the original work was very good and later alterations were poor, one ought to restore the whole back to the original state. If that cannot be done, one might restore to the latest tolerable character. Freeman used as a praiseworthy example St Mary at Stafford, restored by George Gilbert Scott. Of that restoration I shall give a more detailed report somewhat later.

The Cambridge Camden Society in the *Ecclesiologist* of May 1847 reviewed Freeman's pamphlet. Their summing-up is more their own than Freeman's. There are three types of restoration, they wrote: destructive, conservative and eclectic. Destructive would be not to preserve anything, a principle 'universally adopted by our ancestors', conservative is to keep 'the exact details of every piece of ancient work' right down to Tudor. It will be noticed that Georgian was, without even an argument, beyond the pale. Eclectic restoration chooses now to restore, now to remodel. Destructive restoration works towards an 'abstract perfection', without respect for the past. Conservative restoration is the safest method, but eclectic is declared the Camdenian's choice.

In the year of this review the Annual General Meeting of the Society took place in May.[40] Restoration was again discussed. Neale – as he admitted later, for reasons of provocation (after all he was even then only twenty-nine years old) – declared that he would not mind to see Peterborough Cathedral demolished, provided it were to be replaced by a Middle Pointed building 'as good of its sort'. That is of course the extreme of the destructive method. Few at the meeting pronounced themselves in favour of the conservative method. The meeting, as was to be expected, came out as adherents of the eclectic method. Webb was in this lobby, and also Street and Beresford Hope, the moving spirit a few years later behind All Saints, Margaret Street.

In the end the Ecclesiologists' attitude could result in changing a building towards an ideal never in fact realized by the building in the course of its history – 'conferring a religiosity of aspect and arrangement above . . . [its] genuine nature' is what they once called it in 1867,[41] or it could result in no more than a respectful revealing of original parts hidden by later alterations. The former was the rule, the latter the exception.

F. A. Paley, brother of Paley, the North Country architect, and grandson of Paley of the *Evidences*, in 1844 had written a pretty tale to canvass for the latter attitude. The little book dedicated to Salvin, the restorer of the Round Church in Cambridge, is called *The Church Restorers*, and it introduces us first, by way of preamble to Parson Joliffe, a fox-hunting parson who installs a wine-cooler as a font. He is followed by Parson Holdworthy, whose principles are evangelical and who removes the screen, boards off the chancel and puts in an iron stove. Restoration becomes necessary, and the parson calls in Mr Carter, 'a bustling little man' who had built a Swiss villa, an Egyptian cemetery chapel, and a hotel 'in no style at all'. However, his partner has been in Athens, and so the firm must be all right. All this, it need hardly be said, Paley got straight from Pugin. But Parson Holdworthy's son is up in Oxford, where he meets Mr Wilkinson, a graduate of Oxford and an architect. Both Carter and Wilkinson visit the church. Carter walks round whistling, Wilkinson first of all kneels. Holdworthy Jr. and Wilkinson win. Original patterns are recovered and incidentally the pews are removed, encaustic floor tiles are laid, and a stone altar is installed.

So much of Paley and his Letherton Church, and so much of the restoration campaigns of the Ecclesiologists. The result of their efforts, as everyone knows, was church restoration according to their principles on a massive scale. Mr Ferriday, in an excellent paper,[42] reports that in the Diocese of Peterborough alone – and it is not a large diocese – between 1844 and 1874, £539,000 was spent on restoration.

Now the most successful of all large-scale restorers, was Scott, and with him we have reached Act Four.

★   ★   ★

Sir George Gilbert Scott was born in 1811, one year before Pugin. Having started in partnership with a minor architect, Moffatt, on a practice of workhouses, Pugin's writings converted him, not to Catholicism, not even to Anglo-Catholicism – he was a middle-of-the-road man all his life – but to Middle Pointed, to architectural scholarship and to principles of respect for church buildings of the past, a respect, alas, as will be seen presently, which graced his writings more than his doings. The restoration of St Mary at Stafford started in 1841, that of Boston in Lincolnshire in 1843. The cathedrals followed, beginning at Ely in 1847 and going on to Westminster Abbey in 1849, and so to Hereford, Lichfield, Salisbury in the 1850s; Chichester, St David's, Ripon, Chester in the 1860s, Worcester, Exeter, Rochester in the 1870s. And this list is by no means complete.

For the conflict between principles and performance it is enough to look at Stafford and Boston, and Scott's earliest book, characteristically called *A Plea for the faithful Restoration of our Ancient Churches* and published in 1850, but largely the text of a lecture given in 1848. In defence of his activity at Stafford, this is what Scott wrote:

I do not wish to lay it down as a general rule that good taste requires that every alteration which from age to age had been made in our churches should be obliterated, and the whole reduced to its ancient uniformity of style. These varieties are indeed most valuable, as being the standing history of the edifice, from which the date of every alteration and repair may be read as clearly as if it had been verbally recorded; and in many cases the later additions are as valuable specimens of architecture as the remains of the original structure, and merit an equally careful preservation. I even think that if our churches were to be viewed like the ruins of Greece and Rome, only as original monuments from which ancient architecture is to be studied, they would be more valuable in their present condition, however mutilated and decayed, than with any, even the slightest degree of restoration. But taking the more correct view of a church as a building erected for the glory of God and the use of Man (and which must therefore be kept in a proper state of repair) and finding it in such a state of dilapidation that the earlier and later parts – the authentic and the spurious – are alike decayed and all require renovation to render the edifice suitable to its purposes, I think we are then at liberty to exercise our best judgement upon the subject, and if the original parts are found to be 'precious' and the late insertions to be 'vile', I think we should be quite right in giving perpetuity to the one, and in removing the other.[43]

So much for the principle. What Scott actually did is this: he found the church full of galleries, with the pulpit near the west end; and he remedied these two faults. The nave was (and is) early Early English with a Perpendicular clerestory and roof, the chancel and transepts are

*St Mary's, Stafford, before and after restoration by Sir George Gilbert Scott in 1841*

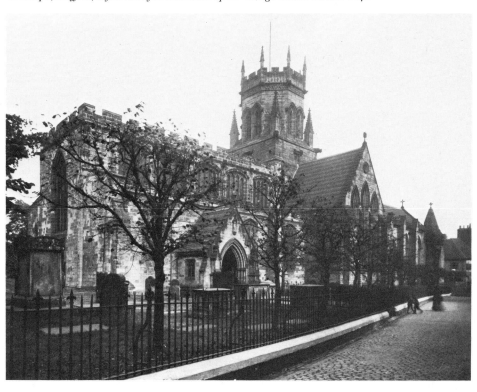

Early English too, but largely of a later phase, and with the upper parts of chancel and south transept of shortly after 1593. These parts 'wilfully mutilated in an age of degenerate taste', as Scott calls it, he restored on quite considerable evidence to the pristine Early English likeness. The evidence was one west lancet. On the strength of this the Perpendicular windows had to disappear. Equally the chancel east wall had a large Perpendicular window and received a group of three lancets. In the north chancel aisle one window was Early English. Scott made a row of matching ones. In the south chancel aisle the same process resulted in Middle Pointed windows, i.e. windows with Geometrical tracery. The clerestory was, of course, adjusted too, and only the north transept was left alone, because money was running out. Scott defended all this against the Rev. J. R. Petit, secretary of the Lichfield Architectural Society and an engaging writer on medieval architecture. Petit argued that 'an architect ought to hesitate long, before he pronounces to be vile and worthless the works of those who lived . . . [in an age] on the decline', and Scott agreed but said that his arguments were 'for the exception, not against the rule' – a typical Scott.

Now Boston:[44]

There is no object on which an architect can be called upon to give an opinion which involves at once such deep interest and such serious responsibility as the restoration of an ancient church. . . . The object of every repair should be the faithful restoration of those features of the original building which yet remain, and their preservation from further injury . . . and no alteration should be attempted which is not the renewal of some ancient feature which has been lost, or absolutely necessary for rendering the building suitable to the present wants of the parishioner; and this should be done in strict conformity with the character and intention of the building.

So far so good. But go to Boston, and you will see and probably admire a large east window in the Decorated style and with gorgeous flowing tracery, and this is entirely by Scott, and was copied from Carlisle Cathedral.

Finding himself in such a situation Scott was bound to feel the need for a more public justification, and so, in his *A Plea for the faithful Restoration of our Ancient Churches*, he came out strongly against 'the torrent of destructiveness' by unscrupulous restoration. 'It is a most lamentable fact, that there has been far more done to obliterate genuine examples of pointed architecture by the tampering caprices of well-meant restoration than . . . by centuries of mutilation and neglect.' Once restoration has started, 'little by little, the conservative principle is departed from, till the whole character and identity of the building is changed' and it has lost 'all its truthfulness'. Instead what shall the restoring architect do? 'As a general rule, it is highly desirable to preserve those vestiges of the growth and history of the building which are indicated by the various styles and irregularities of its parts. . . . Some vestige at least of the oldest

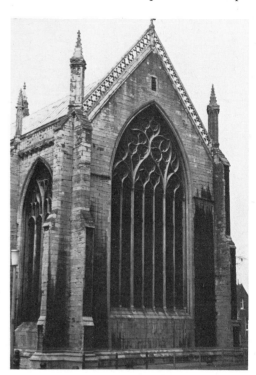

*Boston parish church, east window by Scott, 1843*

portions should always be preserved.' On the other hand the removal of some later parts 'in some instances . . . may be desirable . . . particularly when the later portions are decayed, and the earlier may be restored with absolute certainty'. But the rule should yet be that 'an authentic feature, though late and poor, is more worthy than an earlier though finer part conjecturally restored', and this seems even meant to apply to 'reminiscences of the age of Elizabeth, of James or of the martyred Charles'.

But did it in fact? Nearly always Scott would prefer to 'restore an early form at the cost of removing a later one'. He may assure us that he 'does so with pain', but there is, for example, the completely new rose window in the style of the late twelfth century in the east wall of Oxford Cathedral replacing a fourteenth-century window. And Scott's book contains more ominous remarks. 'An original detail . . . though partially decayed or mutilated, is infinitely more valuable than the most skilful attempt at its restoration', but that should not prevent the architect from replacing 'features which have been actually destroyed by modern mutilations, where they can be indisputably traced'. And even in cases where there is no clue for the replacement, 'let hints be searched for from churches of corresponding age in the same neighbourhood'. This procedure Scott includes among what he calls 'raising the architectural character', and he pleads that when the restorer has to follow the methods called by Freeman 'destructive' and 'eclectic' he should do so with 'warmth and feeling'.

Side by side with Oxford Cathedral there is, for example, the Holy Sepulchre at Northampton and on this I can also quote Scott himself.[45] The following passage was written in 1861:

The primary question is whether or not we aim at bringing it back to its ancient form? I see no difficulty about its external wall: we have evidence enough here to restore with absolute certainty. We may also be able to restore the groining shafts with certainty, though as yet I am not quite decided as to their design, the one which remains presenting some puzzling difficulties. Were these satisfactorily restored, the groining might follow, though with less certainty as to its original design, particularly as regards the section of the transverse ribs, and the manner in which it would rest on the pillars. Before this could be done, however, the form of the original Round would have to be regained, both at the east and west, involving very extensive alterations, including the closing of the tower arch, and those leading into the chancel aisles. When we reach the arcade, with the triforium arches and the clerestory, however, we should be left wholly to conjecture.

And what did he do at Nantwich? The west doorway was Perpendicular, the large window above it Decorated; both are now Middle Pointed. At Cholmondeley the chapel near the house is of the mid-seventeenth century, with a medieval chancel; Scott wanted to match the chancel with a new nave.

But we should not blame Scott too much. For one thing, he enriched cathedrals in the course of his restoration by such fitments as iron screens. He designed them, and Skidmore of Coventry made them. The removal of the screen at Hereford, and the removal and destruction of that at Salisbury, has been sheer vandalism; for these screens are transparent, i.e. no obstacle to views into the chancel, and they are of the highest craftmanship. Secondly, Scott's principles of restoration were those accepted also by the most successful and the most learned French restorer, Viollet-le-Duc, who wrote: 'Restaurer un édifice, ce n'est pas l'entretenir, le réparer ou le refaire, c'est rétablir dans un état complet qui peut n'avoir jamais existé, à un moment donné,'[46] and invented for Clermont-Ferrand Cathedral a whole *Rayonnant*, i.e. Middle Pointed, west front to a fourteenth-century nave – a piece of scholarly conjecture, not of wild fancy as Lord Grimthorpe's, the formidable amateur architect's, west front of St Albans.

And thirdly it must always be remembered that when the Victorian restorers started, our major medieval buildings were still in a state of shocking neglect. The chapter house of Westminster Abbey was filled with files with access by a spiral iron staircase and iron galleries, and at St Albans a public way cut right across the building.

Such arguments may incline us to mercy, but they did not convince that other protagonist in Act Four, Scott's implacable adversary John Ruskin. Ruskin was eight years younger than Scott, seven than Pugin. His *The Seven Lamps of Architecture* was published in 1849, the year after Scott had given his lecture and one year before, quite possibly in self defence against Ruskin, he published the book of the lecture. Ruskin's message was plain enough:

Neither by the public nor by those who have the care of public monuments, is the true meaning of the word *restoration* understood. It means the most total destruction which a building can suffer: a destruction out of which no remnants can be gathered: a destruction accompanied with false descriptions of the thing destroyed. Do not let us deceive ourselves in this important matter; it is impossible, as impossible as to raise the dead, to restore anything that has ever been great or beautiful in architecture. That which I have above insisted upon as the life of the whole, that spirit which is given only by the hand and eye of the workman, can never be recalled. Another spirit may be given by another time, and it is then a new building; but the spirit of the dead workman cannot be summoned up, and commanded to direct other hands, and other thoughts. And as for direct and simple copying, it is palpably impossible. What copying can there be of surfaces that have been worn half an inch down? The whole finish of the work, was in the half inch that is gone; if you attempt to restore that finish, you do it conjecturally; if you copy what is left, granting fidelity to be possible (and what care, or watchfulness, or cost can secure it), how is the new work better than the old? There was yet in the old some life, some mysterious suggestion of what it had been, and of what it had lost; some sweetness in the gentle lines which rain and sun had wrought. There can be none in the brute hardness of the new carving. . . . Do not let us talk then of restoration. The thing is a Lie from beginning to end. You may make a model of a building as you may of a corpse, and your model may have the shell of the old walls within it as your cast might have the skeleton, with what advantage I neither see nor care; but the old building is destroyed, and that more totally and mercilessly than if it had sunk into a heap of dust, or melted into a mass of clay: more has been gleaned out of desolated Nineveh than ever will be out of re-built Milan.[47]

Ruskin never changed his thesis, nor did Scott, and only a few years before Scott died, i.e. in 1874, Ruskin refused the Royal Institute of Architects' gold medal because of 'the destruction under the name of restoration brought about by architects'.[48]

Scott was not alone in putting forward reasons against Ruskin's radicalism. The *Ecclesiologist*[49] wrote: 'We are not artists only: we have a duty to consider the comeliness and decency of God's house.'

But Ruskin made one unexpected convert, the Society of Antiquaries, a body not as a rule sympathetic to radical views. What had happened is this:[50] Ruskin had proposed 'that the Society should . . . manage a Fund for the Preservation of Medieval Buildings'. Ruskin promised £25 a year to it, and held out hopes that friends of his would give more. The Society accepted the idea of the fund and on 11 January 1855 stated as its purpose to embark on a catalogue of ancient buildings and to promote the conservation of ancient buildings 'in the sense of preservation from the ravages of time or negligence, without any attempt to add to, alter or restore'. In due course, or, to be precise, on 1 May 1855, a memorandum was brought out which said this:

The numerous instances of destruction of the character of Ancient Monuments which are taking place under the pretence of Restoration induce the Executive Committee . . . to call the special attention of the Society to the subject in the hope that its influences may be exerted to stop, or at least moderate, the pernicious practice. The evil is an increasing one.

Time and neglect, the memorandum went on, have done less damage than 'the indiscreet zeal for restoration. Restoration may possibly . . . produce good imitation of an ancient work of art; but the original is then falsified, and in its *restored* state it is no longer an example of the art of the period to which it belonged'. In fact 'the more exact the imitation the more it is adapted to mislead posterity'. The committee therefore urge that, except if needed for services, 'no restoration should ever be attempted, otherwise than . . . in the sense of preservation from further injuries. . . . Anything beyond this is untrue in art, unjustifiable in taste, destructive in practice, and wholly opposed to the judgement of the best Archaeologists'. The style makes it likely that Ruskin drafted this actual document. It did not turn events the way Ruskin wished to turn them. On the contrary, the period from 1855 to 1875 was the heyday of restoration on the Scott pattern. Among the foremost restorers were Ewan Christian who, according to Canon Clarke, restored about 350 churches,[51] and J. L. Pearson who worked, for example, on Westminster Abbey and Lincoln, Peterborough and Rochester cathedrals.

★  ★  ★

The year 1877 marks the beginning of Act Five; for 1877 is the year of William Morris's letter to the *Athenaeum*. He wrote on 5 March:[52]

Sir, My eye just now caught the word 'restoration' in the morning paper, and, on looking closer, I saw that this time it is nothing less than the minster of Tewkesbury that is to be destroyed by Sir Gilbert Scott. Is it altogether too late to do something to save it – it and whatever else of beautiful or historical is still left to us on the sites of the ancient buildings we were once so famous for? Would it not be of some use once for all, and with the least delay possible, to set on foot an association for the purpose of watching over and protecting these relics, which, scanty as they are now become, are still wonderful treasures, all the more priceless in this age of the world, when the newly-invented study of living history is the chief joy of so many of our lives?

Your paper has so steadily and courageously opposed itself to those acts of barbarism which the modern architect, parson, and squire call 'restoration', that it would be waste of words to enlarge here on the ruin that has been wrought by their hands; but for the saving of what is left, I think I may write a word of encouragement, and say that you by no means stand alone in the matter, and that there are many thoughtful people who would be glad to sacrifice time, money and comfort in defence of those ancient monuments:

besides, though I admit that the architects are with very few exceptions, hopeless, because interest, habit, and ignorance bind them, and that the clergy are hopeless, because their order, habit and an ignorance yet grosser, bind them; still there must be many people whose ignorance is accidental rather than inveterate, whose good sense could surely be touched if it were clearly put to them that they were destroying what they, or, more surely still, their sons and sons' sons, would one day fervently long for, and which no wealth or energy could ever buy again for them.

What I wish for, therefore, is that an association should be set on foot to keep a watch on old monuments, to protect against all 'restoration' that means  more than keeping out wind and weather, and by all means, literary and other, to awaken a feeling that our ancient buildings are not mere ecclesiastical toys, but sacred monuments of the nation's growth and hope.

The effect was instantaneous. Among the first committee members were the following – twenty-five out of eighty-eight – in alphabetical order: Bentley (of Westminster Cathedral), Stopford Brooke, Carlyle, J. Comyns Carr (of Bedford Park), Professor Colvin (Slade Professor), de Morgan, Richard Doyle, J. P. Heseltine (the collector), Holman Hunt, Burne-Jones, Charles Keene, Sir John Lubbock, H. Stacey Marks, Coventry Patmore, Mark Pattison, E. R. Robson (the schools' architect), Ruskin, W. Bell Scott, Leslie Stephen, J. J. Stevenson, Alma Tadema, Canon Venables (the archaeologist), Thomas Wardle (Morris's friend, the dyer of Leek) and Philip Webb. And among the earliest members in addition the following deserve the record: John Willis Clark (of Cambridge), Sir C. W. Dilke, the Rev. Whitwell Elwin (the amateur architect), Birkett Foster, Charles Hadfield (the Catholic architect), John Honeyman (a Glasgow architect), Arthur Hughes (the Pre-Raphaelite painter), L. A. Ionides, Millais, Fairfax Murray (of Siena), Hungerford Pollen, William Rossetti, Marcus Stone, G. F. Watts – the number of painters is remarkable. They seem to have respected old buildings more than the architects.

Secretary of the new society of course was Morris. Morris had in fact been convinced by Ruskin's attitude to restoration when he was still very young: of Dreux, for example, he wrote in 1855 'Deo gratias not yet restored'.[53] His love, of course, belonged wholly to the Middle Ages. Of the Renaissance he wrote: 'I deny it that name.'[54] Yet as a true preservationist he did not want to confine protection to one style or one period. So on 17 April 1878 he wrote to *The Times*:[55]

Sir: The question asked by Lord Houghton in the House of Lords on Thursday elicited from the Bishop of London an acknowledgment that the scheme proposed some few years back for the wholesale removal of the City churches is continuing its destructive course unimpeded. Four more churches are to be sacrificed to the Mammon-worship and want of taste of this great city. Last year witnessed the destruction of the fine church of St Michael's Queenhithe, and All Hallows, Bread Street, which bore upon its walls the inscription stating that Milton had been baptized there. St Dionis Backchurch, a remarkable building by Wren, is now in course of destruction, while within the last ten years the beautiful church of St Antholin, with its charming spire, and the skilfully designed little church of St Mildred in the Poultry, All Hallows, Staining (except its tower), St James's, Duke Place, St Benet, Gracechurch, with its picturesque steeple, the tower and vestibule of All Hallows-the-Great, Thames Street, have all disappeared. Those for the removal of which a Commission has now been issued are as follows: St Margaret Pattens, Rood Lane; St George, Botolph Lane; St Matthew, Friday Street; and St Mildred, Bread Street, all works of Wren, and two of them, St Mildred, Bread Street, and St Margaret Pattens, possessing spires of singularly original and beautiful design. It must not be supposed that these are the only churches which are in danger, but their proposed destruction serves to show the fate which sooner or later is in store for the whole of Wren's churches in this city, unless Englishmen can be awakened, and by strong and earnest protest show the ecclesiastical authorities that they will not tamely submit to this outrageous and monstrous barbarity.

From an art point of view the loss of these buildings will be irreparable, for Wren's churches form a distinct link in the history of the ecclesiastical art of this country.

Many persons suppose that by preserving St Paul's Cathedral, that architect's great masterpiece, enough will be left to illustrate his views upon ecclesiastical architecture, but this is far from being the case. For, grand as St Paul's undoubtedly is, it is only one of a class of buildings common enough on the Continent – imitations of St Peter's, Rome. In fact, St Paul's can scarcely be looked upon as an English design, but, rather, as an English rendering of the great Italian original, whereas the City churches are examples of purely English Renaissance architecture as applied to ecclesiastical purposes, and illustrate a style of architecture peculiar not only to this country but even to this city, and when they are destroyed the peculiar phase of architecture which they exhibit will have ceased to exist, and nothing will be left to record it. The Continent possesses nothing in the least resembling our City churches, and the fact that they are all found in such close proximity to one another only serves to make them the more valuable for purposes of study. One great merit which they possess is shown by the fact that, though they are diminutive in point of size, scarcely any one of them being above 80 ft long, they possess a dignity of proportion, a masterly treatment as to scale, which renders them far more imposing than many buildings double and treble their dimensions; the relation which they bear to each other and to the great Cathedral which they surround, enhancing by their thin taper spires the importance of the majestic dome, and relieving the dullness and monotony of the general sky line of the City, all serve as unanswerable arguments for their preservation. Surely an opulent city, the capital of the commercial world, can afford some small sacrifice to spare these beautiful buildings the little plots of ground upon which they stand. Is it absolutely necessary that every scrap of space in the City should be devoted to money-making, and are religion, sacred memories, recollections of the great dead, memorials of the past, works of England's greatest architect, to be banished from this wealthy City? If so, alas for our pretended love of art; alas for the English feeling of reverence of which we hear so much; alas for those who are to come after us, whom we shall have robbed of works of art which it was our duty to hand down to them uninjured and unimpaired; alas for ourselves, who will be looked upon by foreign nations and by our own posterity as the only people who have ever lived, who, possessing no architecture of their own, have made themselves remarkable for the destruction of the buildings of their forefathers. I am, Sir, Your obedient servant, William Morris.

Morris's and his friends' confessions of faith in Ruskin's *j'accuse* had immediate effects. One was that within the walls of the Royal Institute of British Architects at a meeting, still in 1877, a fellow architect attacked Scott as a restorer. He was J. J. Stevenson, one of the earliest protagonists of the so-called Queen Anne Revival.[56] He said: 'It is a delusion of restorers that their new work, because it is correctly medieval in style, is of any historical value,' and he referred as examples to the removal of pews and galleries, the removing of plaster from walls – the scraping which led to the term 'Anti-Scrape', the nickname of Morris's Society – the changes of roof-pitch from the Perpendicular to the steeper Middle Pointed angle, and to the removal of whole buildings, as at Balliol College in Oxford. The rebuttals to Stevenson's address were furious. Beresford Hope called it intellectual barbarism, Ferrey agreed and Scott himself complained that Stevenson's initial description of an unrestored church was *couleur de rose* in the face of all real evidence. He had a point there, as we have seen, but the battle was lost.

He died in 1878, and in 1884 Morris referred to him as 'the happily dead dog.'[57] Morris and the Anti-Scrape could indeed rejoice in victory. Medieval evidence is now sacrosanct; so is Tudor, Stuart and Georgian – though the redundance of so many hundreds of churches all over the country will pose desperate problems to the preservers and those who do or ought to provide money for preservation. But the Victorian Age is far less well protected against depredations. In other pages of this book the weakness of legislation and government action will be shown up. Here I will end with one special problem, not without irony in our context. The Victorian restorers removed 'original' features, Perpendicular and later, and especially Georgian, and we tell them they were vandals. What they put in their stead a hundred years ago, should not that now be as sacrosanct as the Georgian pieces a hundred years old when they removed them? Should we not watch that we don't become the incorrigible vandals of a century from today? Scott's and Skidmore's screens, for example, to which I have already referred, ought to be protected against the zeal of today's Ecclesiologists, the men of the Liturgical Movement who just like their predecessors plead for destruction in the name of worship. Surely, with some sympathetic effort the aim of closer participation in the service can be achieved without sweeping away what is of architectural value. It may be a challenge, but challenge can be a stimulus to architects and clients alike.

# JOHN BETJEMAN

*Holly Village, Highgate West Hill, by Alfred Darbyshire*

# III   A preservationist's progress

HARM has been done to the cause of architecture by the division of people into preservationists and destroyers. The truth is there is a bit of each in all of us. Since 1929 I have been engaged in battles with local authorities almost always with the aid of preservation societies. One is not a lone figure fighting to stop the pulling down and cutting down of what is worth looking at. One is a member of a rapidly increasing band of men of good will; at least so I like to think.

There are those who say that to want to preserve anything is a confession of defeat, yet the Turks seem to have spared many Greek and Roman temples and the Italians to have adapted some to Christian worship. In our own country those who completed the nave of Westminster Abbey did so in the later Middle Ages in the early Gothic style in which it was originally built centuries before. When things have been planted with care and skill and with regard to neighbours, whether these are trees or buildings, the plant has about it a reverence which makes its destruction a crime, even if that crime is committed in the name of high finance. The only conquering force on the side of architectural preservation is affection for the buildings worth preserving. Taste changes, so that the foundation of the Victorian Society is considered by some elderly people as an unnecessary obstacle invented by intellectuals who like wax fruit and whatnots in the Portobello Road.

What makes you like architecture are the things you have seen and reacted to as a child. Now is the time, therefore, to be autobiographical. The earliest buildings I remember were those in Highgate West Hill, and I did not realize that some of them were charming Georgian. I thought some very tall buildings, Pimlico-style near our house, were very ugly. One of them was lived in by some people called Garnett. I think they were the British Museum lot, and I used to call out 'Ugly Garnetts,' I remember; because of the architecture, not because of them – they were very nice people. And then I remember terror at that job by Darbyshire at the bottom of West Hill, Holly Village, with those curious spikes against the skyline in a Gothic style. And I remember thinking (my earliest reminiscences, I think, of London architecture) that anything in grey or stock brick was rather ugly and that red brick was beautiful. I remember my father telling me that this was not so. We used to go for walks in Kentish Town which then had little cottages in it – Middlesex cottages, with those crinkly tiles you get in Middlesex. Then there rose up between Parliament Hill Fields and Gospel Oak Station a thing called Glenhurst Avenue which had bow-windowed houses in red brick, like Metroland. I thought these were beautiful, and my father told me they were awful. I now see that he was right.

The next thing I recall that first moved me to realize that there was something more than just surface in architecture was *The Ghost Stories of an Antiquary*, by M. R. James. Those stories bring out the Norfolk landscape, Perpendicular churches, Georgian squires' houses in red brick, Strawberry Hill Gothick, mezzotints and the eighteenth century as well as the Middle Ages – and with that touch of horror which is essential to keep one's attention.

I was extraordinarily lucky at my private school. At the Dragon's School at Oxford I was allowed to look round churches and colleges, on my own and with friends and to hear C. C. Lynam, 'the Skipper' as he was called, tell us those stories by M. R. James, as though they had happened to himself. After that, my next architectural interest was away from Gothic, which, I was told, was the only style. I can remember a book on architecture in the *Shown to the Children Series* published by T. E. and C. Jack. It ran through the whole lot – Norm., Dec., E.E., Perp., and then a quick bit about St Paul's, and then it said, 'What is your favourite style? Does it begin with a G?' By then mine didn't, but it does now.

I was sent to Marlborough, but I spent a lot of my holidays in London and I found the City churches. There were a lot more of them then than there are now. I have always preferred unimportant things to ones which are well known, and so I found churches which have since been pulled down, with box-pews in them and clear glass windows, and very lazy rectors, and very uncooperative churchwardens, such as St Catherine Coleman, and places which have long disappeared.

It was a great experience, and it led me on to the next interest. There was then a second-hand bookshop in every borough and many in the Borough of St Pancras. I bought *Metropolitan Improvements* by Thomas H. Shepherd, steel-engravings of London in the 1820s (the sort of things that are now tinted in by watercolour and put on to dinner mats). Then you could buy the whole book for half-a-crown, because steel-engravings were not thought anything, and for a few shillings you could still buy coloured aquatint books. These led me to looking at the Greek Revival, and then my eyes were opened by looking at a book called *Monumental Classic Architecture in Great Britain and Ireland* by A. E. Richardson, 1912, Batsford. That was folio with whacking great sepia photographs by Bedford Lemere. Those pictures opened up a world to me that I did not know existed – that you could go on beyond Sir Christopher Wren and even admire Somerset House, and still more the Greek Revival, and notice things like Waterloo Bridge, and the British Museum, and branches of the Bank of England, in the Romano-Greek style, in Bristol and Birmingham.

That led me on to go to Oxford where naturally I reacted against the Greek Revival, and certainly against genuine Gothic, which merely seemed funny and rather pathetic. Nice old people in knee-breeches who were members of the Art-Workers' Guild seemed the kind of people who would be expected to like it, but we were superior. I started to like the Gothick Revival with a 'k' as hinted at in M. R. James's stories, and I even began to like the Gothic Revival as seen in Oxford, when it was Perpendicular revival of the 1820s and 30s. I could now see the merits of the Houses of Parliament. And this was in the 1920s, when of course the prevailing taste was all in favour of the classical, and being as like Wren as possible. Sir Reginald Blomfield told us what we ought to like, and he said that Nash was false, because he used stucco, and he made a great design for pulling down Carlton House Terrace, and putting in its place an enlarged Swan and Edgar's.

When, after having been a schoolmaster, I was on the *Architectural Review* in a subsidiary position, I used to have to go round to the architects, and collect their drawings. That was when we discovered about this terrible plan of Sir Reginald's to pull down Carlton House Terrace. I went to see Lutyens, who showed me with a pencil and a penny how to turn a moulding from half a pipe into a living curve, by just stopping it being a quarter or a half and making it between the two. And I met Sir Edwin Cooper, who seemed to me rough-spoken. Then I found Mr Voysey, living in a little flat over Rumpelmayers, in St James's Street, where Madame Prunier now lives.

On the *Architectural Review* there were wonderful people. I remember an angry young man coming on a little later than me, called Gordon, because his surname was Richards. You all know him now as Jim Richards. And also P. Morton Shand, who in those days told us all who were the good modern architects abroad, and we copied them. There was, on the other paper, a man called John Summerson – still to me the best writer living on architecture – in those days (just as he is now) diffident, and cool and rather detached. The other paper was the *Architect and Building News*, but he used to write reviews for the *Architectural Review* under the name of Coolmore, which was apparently an estate owned by his mother's family in Ireland. Ever since then I have called that great man Coolmore, because it does rather describe him. He stops over-enthusiasm. I think I have learnt more from him than from anybody else except two people: Frederick Etchells, FRIBA, who built Crawfords at Holborn (because poor old Welch of Welch and Landor could not get it finished properly), and translated Corbusier; and the father of us all, as Kenneth Clark has described him – Goodhart-Rendel, whose book, *English Architecture since the Regency*, 1953, is still to me like St Paul's Epistles: you can find more and more in it every time you turn back to it.

When I founded the *Shell Guides* in 1933, it was with the idea of counteracting the antiquarian, Gothic effect of the *Little Guides*, published by Methuen, and making people interested in Georgian. Even in the eighteenth century there had been a hankering for the Middle Ages. In fact, as Sir Nikolaus has shown, it is hard to draw a line between Gothic Survival and early Gothic Revival. By 1877 the Gothic Revivalists had gone far enough. Morris and his friends did not like to see plaster taken off the walls of churches, whether inside or out, in order to display rough stone which the masons would have been ashamed to present to public gaze. They also delighted, as the poet Crabbe had done, in the texture of time. Hair-splitting differences about whether Decorated was purer than Perp seemed to them trivial. Churches were not the only buildings to be preserved, but manor houses, barns and farm buildings and market halls as well; particularly in the limestone districts where they had endured the weather. Gradually the seventeenth century and the crude attempts at classical motifs made in the latter part of the sixteenth century came into favour, just as had its literature.

One forgets today how rich England was in undisturbed villages, where streets wandered out into commons and woodland; how there were duckponds beside roads and horse-troughs beside highways, and how away from the railway lines there was a country silence so deep that it went back to Chaucer. It may be seen even at the beginning of the present century in the large photogravure books published by Batsford and written by people like Gotch, Garner and Stratton and Macartney, and in the colour-plate books on the different counties published by A. & C. Black, where hens cross village streets and dogs and children play in front of cottage doors in paintings by Helen Allingham. There seemed then to be so much unspoiled country that we could easily have spared some of it for building in order to bring fresh air to the pale mechanics of the industrial North. The warm-hearted social-ism of William Morris, the high-mindedness of such men as Barry Parker and Raymond Unwin, the care for traditional ways of building and for handicrafts shown by the SPAB and the Art Workers' Guild, produced the back to nature element in preservation which goes with vegetarianism, Norfolk jackets, saxe-blue shirts and a tie with a ring in it.

There was already in existence the oldest of the preservation societies concerned with the saving of commons and footpaths, to whose vision, along with that of the Metropolitan Board of Works, we owe open spaces near London like Hampstead Heath. The National Trust was founded in 1895; it was started in the Lake District. The coordination of many local preservation societies and of the commons and footpaths societies resulted in the Council for the Preservation of Rural England, which was started in 1926. Guy Dawber (1861–1938), the architect of so many Cotswold-like cottages and country houses, who did so much for the preservation of his native King's Lynn, and Patrick Abercrombie (1879–1957), the famous town planner, were the leading spirits. They were joined by Clough Williams-Ellis. The last-named as a propagandist first made me see in his book *The Pleasures of Architecture*, London, 1924, how some buildings could be funny. Still more effective was his campaign against hoardings and petrol stations and the frightful advertising in the countryside. His *England and the Octopus*, London, 1928, with its photographs of ruination of landscape scenery and his cautionary guides to various districts, were a great awakening for many people; so was the work for the SCAPA Society – founded to control outdoor advertising. Indeed calling the country the 'countryside', a delightful suburbanism, dates, I think, from the 1920s and has a flavour of the garden city about it. Young architects in the 1920s were much given to wearing tweeds and plus-fours, unlike the urbane city-type architects of Edwardian days. This interest in the countryside meant that buildings were thought of again in relation to their settings, as they had been in the late eighteenth and early nineteenth centuries. Hitherto guide books and the Town Clerk's brochure still confined their remarks to the ancientness of a building, disregarding its setting and rarely mentioning over-restoration. The *Shell Guides* were founded primarily to draw attention to Georgian and early Victorian architecture and to deplore over-restoration. The Royal Commission on Historical Monuments was founded in 1908. It was to record monuments from the earliest times until 1700, a limit which was later extended to 1714. This meant that a whole army of archaeologists was engaged in listing and illustrating earthworks and vestigial foundations. It continues to do so today. In the Middlesex volume published in the 1930s, Robert Adam's Syon House had to be described as 'a modern building, incorporating an undercroft of Henry V'. Its only illustration of Syon showed this bit of cellar. The limit has since been extended into the nineteenth century, but with work of such thoroughness at the government's expense, it is naturally hard to know what to exclude and what to include. In my opinion there should be no dateline, only an 'eye' line.

The urbane architects such as Arthur J. Davis, the excellent designer of the Ritz, Sir Reginald Blomfield and Sir Herbert Baker, were keen on the preservation of Georgian buildings. Almost the first effort in this direction occurred at the height of the Gothic Revival, when there were proposals to pull down the Georgian brick parish church of Hampstead in 1874, and a petition against such vandalism was signed by Butterfield, J. P. Seddon and Alfred Waterhouse. The chief promoters of the protest were George Gilbert Scott Junior and G. F. Bodley. Possibly because of their newly discovered affection for Georgian, Hampstead parish church had in its congregation the architects Basil Champneys, Reginald

Blomfield and those two loyal High Churchmen, Norman Shaw and Temple Moore. When the Bishop of London, shortly after World War I, proposed to demolish nineteen City churches, the LCC, as it then was, published an effective booklet illustrated with photographs, deploring the proposals and praising the churches that were to be demolished. J. C. Squire, too, wrote a fine poem of protest.

Even so, until the late 1920s, while in the public estimation Wren was to be admired, architects later than he were hardly thought of as comparable. As for Regency architecture and the stucco crescents and terraces in places like Cheltenham, Brighton, Sidmouth, Devonport, Tenby and around Regent's Park, London – they were regarded as false and late. The first battle I remember being engaged in publicly was the effort to save Rennie's superb Waterloo Bridge from destruction by the LCC under Herbert Morrison, in the name of traffic widening. An effective letter to *The Times* from Sir Herbert Baker mentioned how carefully this bridge of Cornish granite, with coupled Doric columns between elliptical arches, was designed to act as a plinth to Somerset House when viewed from Westminster. Sir Giles Gilbert Scott's modern bridge fails to do this. Though impressive in itself, it is wider than necessary and disregards Somerset House. It was not until many years later I discovered that the destruction of Waterloo Bridge was brought about through rival factions in politics in the LCC. About this time also was the scandal of Carlton House Terrace, when Sir Reginald Blomfield, hitherto thought of as an ally in the cause of Georgian architecture, proposed to rebuild Carlton House Terrace in Portland stone and a French Renaissance style to match his new Regent Street. A foretaste of it is the Pinchin Johnson building (1932–34) in Carlton Gardens. The

*Waterloo Bridge, by Rennie, demolished 1939*

*The Imperial Institute, London, by T. E. Collcutt. The tower on the right was saved when the rest was demolished*

*Daily Mirror* called Blomfield's design for a new Carlton House Terrace 'a monster of gleaming ugliness'. Blomfield said that stucco was false and John Nash not a good architect.

The pioneer popular book on the subject going into whole groups of buildings instead of the individual masterpiece was *Good and Bad Manners in Architecture*, 1924, by A. Trystan Edwards. In the late 20s and early 30s, the *Architectural Review* ran campaigns to save Georgian buildings, and the greatest campaigner of all was Robert Byron, who with his friend Lord Rosse founded the Georgian Group in 1937, with Lord Derwent as its first chairman. It was Robert Byron who first made the phrase 'amenities' popular. It would be interesting to know who was the inventor of its useful successor 'the environment'.

After the war that far-seeing and too unregarded politician and aesthete, Duncan Sandys, realized that though we had plenty of voluntary societies for preserving the countryside, such as the National Trust and the CPRE, and that though we had many local preservation societies, which were springing up in every town and county, there was a limit to the money available to save what was left worth looking at.

The greatest enemy was, of course, the developer, and he was generally backed by the banks and the insurance companies and would sometimes pay lip service to a street he was going to destroy, and shed crocodile tears over his acres of destruction. Duncan Sandys thought that now was the time to enlist the sympathies of big business on the side of the preservation of what Thomas Sharp, a pioneer of good planning, called 'the townscape'. Duncan Sandys had already opposed the building of high blocks around St Paul's, and had long had an eye for architecture. He founded the Civic Trust in 1957, having first sounded the reactions of big business. It was to do for towns what the National Trust did for houses and their parks and gardens.

Londoners know some of the major post-war crimes. Of these the worst was the removal of the Imperial Institute and the splendid range of South Kensington buildings by the most eminent architects of mid- and later Victorian times by London University. Committees of dons are never good as committees of taste. Committees of taste are only of use as brakes on destruction; they cannot design anything. They hastened the destruction of London's noblest Victorian buildings and they did this in the name of learning and science. Another appalling crime was the destruction of P. C. Hardwick's Great Hall and Propylaeum at Euston Station, the triumphant entrance-hall portico to the first trunk railway in the world. It has been replaced by an inconvenient, undistinguished building, detested by passengers and taxi drivers alike and still given the cold shoulder by public transport. Equally bad was the destruction by the Corporation of the City of London of J. B. Bunning's Coal Exchange, whose cast-iron interior and ingenious corner treatment in Portland stone on a prominent site in the City, made it both original and impressive within and without. The Corporation displayed a cynicism and duplicity worthy of a small town. Great urgency to destroy the Coal Exchange was expressed. Its site is still an untidy car park. What has gone on in London was going on in most of our old towns and cities, particularly in Bristol, Birmingham, Liverpool and Newcastle-on-Tyne. In fact it might be said that more destruction to English cities and towns was wrought by so-called modern architects than by German bombs.

All these destroyed London buildings were constructed in the reign of Queen Victoria. It was natural that a Victorian Society should come into being, however late in the day. It was founded by Lady Rosse and Mr Christopher Hussey; and the late Lord Esher, wisest and most catholic-minded of men, became its first chairman, combining that role with the chairmanship of the SPAB. William Morris would have approved the action. To preserve the best Victorian today is to be what Anti-Scrape was a century before. A sad thing happened in the mid-1930s when the *Architectural Review*, an ally in the battle for preservation, took on the cause of what has come to be called contemporary architecture, that is to say high-rise buildings for high finance. This need not be confused

*The Coal Exchange, Lower Thames Street, by J. B. Bunning, 1846–49, demolished 1962*

with the Bauhaus architecture, though there are many adventurers in consortia of commercial architects, who pretend to be the successors of Gropius and his school. Centrepoint is a good example of their work. Government departments, notably the new Department of the Environment, and architectural journalists in the national dailies and local weeklies have been the greatest allies in the fight to save what is worth looking at from the past and to open people's eyes to architecture.

Immediately if one talks about good work by politicians, one is accused of political bias. I like to think that I have none, but recall with pleasure the work of Nigel Birch (Lord Rhyl), in the Conservative government. I always remember that it was Richard Crossman who saved the Ritz Hotel from demolition and his Parliamentary Private Secretary, Lord Kennet, who with him and later, with Anthony Crosland, did so much for preserving buildings as groups, not as isolated museum pieces. In fact, the Labour government in Whitehall had a better record aesthetically than its representatives on local authorities. Now we have the Department of the Environment, a strong ally in keeping the balance between destruction and preservation. The Department of the Environment has three virtues, faith, hope and charity, and to me the greatest of these is hope.

'Gentlemen, let us get our priorities right! Historic buildings must not be allowed to stand in the way of expensive accommodation for the tourists who come to see these historic buildings!'

'All over the country the grime, muddle and decay of our Victorian heritage is being replaced and the quality of urban life uplifted' – Harold Wilson

# IV  What should we preserve?

*'Time, like an ever-rolling stream,*
*Bears all its sons away;*
*They fly forgotten, as a dream*
*Dies at the opening day'*

—but not, invariably, their handiwork. *Ars longa, vita brevis:* Ictinus and Sir Gilbert Scott are both in their graves, but the Parthenon and St Pancras are with us still. It is my purpose to consider for a moment what our attitude to the architectural achievements of the past – and not just to the acknowledged masterpieces – should be and what action may be expected to arise from it.

The subject falls naturally, I think, into two parts. First, there is the question of what we should preserve, and, second, the question of how we should preserve it; and I shall deal with them in that order.

When a building has survived its original functional usefulness – but first let us be quite sure that it has; for we all know of cases of cottages which could be rendered perfectly comfortable at a quarter the cost of a new semi-detached which are yet ruthlessly swept away in the name of economy – then there are three grounds, and only three, on which we are logically entitled to press for its preservation: of its own intrinsic aesthetic merit, of *pietas*, of its scenic usefulness.

Of these it is the first upon which agreement is most difficult to reach. For no yardstick of aesthetic judgment is of universal validity; time and distance both produce the strangest reversals. No educated person would today contemplate the destruction of Chartres with equanimity, but in the eighteenth century many would have regarded it as welcome deliverance too long delayed. And can we be certain that the obvious necessity for preserving the temple of Paestum would be self-evident to one brought up in the shadow of the Angkor Vat?

However, the consciousness that all judgments on such matters are relative does not absolve us from making them. Moreover, we are now, thanks largely to cheap printing and photography – which as Monsieur André Malraux has so brilliantly shown in *Le Musée Imaginaire* have widened our sensibility to almost universal dimensions – in a far better position than ever before to reach some measure of agreement.

At least on works of a reasonable antiquity; to those of the last 150 years individual reactions will continue to be unpredictable. Perfect harmony of views on the preservation of, say, a church by Street is unlikely to be achieved by Dr Gropius and Sir John Betjeman; and while many regarded Mackintosh's tea-rooms as the fairest jewel in Glasgow's crown, their disappearance left others comparatively unmoved. In such circumstances it is our duty to bear one or two considerations firmly in mind when pronouncing judgment. First, then, we must bear in mind that there are degrees of value, and economic necessity frequently imposes a choice. Therefore before we set up a howl in defence of some admirable but far from unique group of cottages or a Queen Anne rectory, let us always reflect whether or not our action is going to prejudice our chances of stopping the demolition of some acknowledged masterpiece threatened at a later date. Second, let us always beware of the uncertainty of private judgment, remembering that what to us may be without merit may well prove to posterity, who can view it in perspective, of considerable value. Thirdly, although the antiquarian heresy is far less widespread now than when Sir John Betjeman first defined it, it is by no means dead, and the confusion between antiquity and merit is still a common enough threat to sound judgment.

On the second ground for appeal – that of *pietas* – a far greater measure of agreement is likely in most cases to be attained. I here use the Latin word as possessing a rather wider significance than its English equivalent, and I mean by it, in its application to architecture, an emotion widely diffused, unaesthetic and comprehensible only in the light of a people's proper consciousness of their past. In many cases, perhaps, the buildings which evoke it will justify their continued existence also on aesthetic grounds, but not always. Take, for instance, the Tower of London. To a detached view it is simply an injudiciously restored, rather provincial example of twelfth-century functionalism, less offensive than the power station across the way because smaller and unselfconscious. Nevertheless I should be among the first to sign a protest against its demolition and I imagine that most of you would be alongside me in the queue.

Such a reaction, however much it may owe to a youthful absorption in the colourful prose of the late Harrison Ainsworth, is in my view right and proper; and, responding to some of the deepest feelings of the human race, is not to be dismissed as pure sentimentality. How moving, still, are the few monolithic pillars of the Temple of Hera which the Greeks, the least sentimental of peoples, piously left untouched in the very centre of Olympia where every generation did its best to outstrip its predecessors in the scale and sumptuousness of its rebuilding!

However, let us at once admit that such sentiments should be kept strictly within bounds, and never, never exploited for propaganda purposes. The classic and most terrifying example of what is likely to happen if such considerations are disregarded is provided by the present state of Rome. Here during the Fascist régime accumulations of the architectural relics of ten centuries – many of them incidentally evocative in the highest degree of true *pietas* – were too often ruthlessly swept aside in order to expose some dreary symbol of a vulgar past in the vain hope of stimulating enthusiasm for an even vulgarer present. While we may be right in thinking that we are as a nation temperamentally inhibited from such ridiculous performances, we may yet fall into the same error from sentimentality or misplaced enthusiasm for the archaic.

Some years before the war I was concerned in an effort, initiated by that tireless defender of architectural merit to whom all of us are so much indebted, the late Robert Byron, and successful as it turned out, to save Varley House, that handsome eighteenth-century mansion opposite the House of Lords. Among the many fallacious arguments used in favour of its destruction was one, heavily backed, I am sorry to say, by the then Archibishop of Canterbury, that we should at last be afforded a full view of the old medieval jewel house of Westminster Abbey. Upon inspection this proved to be a cube of poorly dressed masonry, not dissimilar in silhouette to those mysterious brick erections in which the Central Electricity Board conceal their transformers or power units. Its aesthetic value was nil; its functional adequacy, judging from the small amount of medieval jewels that has survived, must long ago have been found wanting. Its emotional appeal, as indicated by a total lack of reference to it for a millennium, must have been almost confined to the Archbishop and a handful of archaeologists. And yet for its sake we were being asked to sacrifice a building the retention of which was not only to a fair degree justified on its own aesthetic merits, but provided the most excellent example of my third category of exemptions from destruction, that of those buildings which fulfil a vital role in the landscape.

Of all three of our grounds for defence this is the most difficult upon which to take a stand and by no means the least important. For the number of people who consciously realize the vital part played by one small unit in landscape or an architectural ensemble from which they consciously derive pleasure is always very small. Conscious awareness only comes, alas, when the effect has been ruined by the disappearance of the unit in question. It is, largely, a question of scale and contrast and as such not amenable to generalization. I will therefore confine myself to concrete examples. In the case of Varley House it will, I think, become obvious upon reflection by any person of sensibility standing in Parliament Square and looking upstream towards Millbank, first how much the height and vertical emphasis of the Victoria Tower is increased by the low façade of Varley House, and secondly how greatly the romantic exuberance of Barry and Pugin's great work gains by contrast with the restraint and unenthusiastic classicism of its tiny neighbour across the road. And finally one becomes aware that Varley House acts as a most valuable non-conductor, as it were, between the sixteenth-century Gothic of Henry VII's Chapel and the Victorian version of Perpendicular opposite, both of which would stand to lose from the close proximity of each other were it to be destroyed.

It is in this connection that the practising architect can be of the greatest assistance if he will but bear in mind how much the effect of even the most excellent building can be enhanced by a carefully preserved neighbour. Let me give you a striking and familiar example. Some years ago Dr Sigfried Giedion, in the course of one of his interesting lectures on modern architecture, threw upon the screen a photograph of the Rockefeller Center, the severe beauty and simple structure of which we were, quite rightly, exhorted to admire. But the photographer had cunningly included in his plate the adorned steeple and fretted roof of a neighbouring Neo-Gothic church on Fifth Avenue. Afterwards, at question time, I asked the lecturer if he did not think that some of the effect created by this undoubtedly impressive but not outstandingly subtle building was in this photograph due to the happy inclusion of its humble neighbour? My point was not at that time quite fully appreciated – perhaps due to some slight unfamiliarity with the English language, perhaps not – but it is nevertheless one which I still consider was worth making.

That the building to be preserved for these reasons is not itself of any great merit is beside the point; its function in the scheme of things has become quite different from its original one and such considerations are, therefore, pointless. For example, that dreary little church in Grosvenor Road would hardly be mourned for its own sake by the most besotted Goth, yet its continued existence is to be hoped for, for the sake of the role it plays in the totally new landscape created by the vast housing project immediately behind it.

Having thus briefly considered the only three arguments for preservation which seem to me justifiable, I should like for a moment to discuss one that I do not. No building lacking aesthetic merit, not evoking a genuine *pietas*, and playing no part in the landscape should be allowed to occupy a site needed for something else solely on the grounds that it is unique. One of the few indisputable benefits which modern science has afforded us is that of making full and accurate records. Therefore it is not sufficient to say that this stretch of wall must be preserved because it is the only existing example of such and such a form of bonding dating from the Roman occupation. So what? we can reply. Now that we know that the Romans did build in this particular way, measure it, photograph it and pull it down. For in order to preserve what should be preserved we must, at all costs, be clear-headed about our motives. We must realize that we are deeply thankful that Westminster Hall escaped the bombing not because it is the largest fourteenth-century open timber roof in the world, but because it is a work of supreme architectural merit, deeply embedded at the very heart of our history, playing a vital role in the architectural ensemble of Parliament, St Margaret's and the Abbey.

Having thus inadequately defined the grounds on which we are entitled to preserve, I should like in the space which remains to me to say something on how I consider preservation should be undertaken. This is the more difficult owing to the virtual impossibility of generalizing; every old building presents peculiar problems and demands individual treatment. One can, therefore, only attempt to define the rough outline of the problem and confine oneself to the negative role of saying what on no account must be done.

When at the beginning of this essay I indicated that the hymn-writer's observations on the transitoriness of human beings did not apply to their artifacts I was, of course, speaking relatively. Architecture, unlike painting and to a certain extent sculpture, does, save in the absolute sense, exist in time. It suffers the effects of wind and weather, and the additions and alterations of man. It may be frozen music, but it melts. And this process is by no means invariably a disadvantage, and its operation should always be foreseen by architects; for at a certain point in time even the greatest architecture ceases to be completely architecture and becomes partially landscape. Sometimes the wheel at last turns full circle; the pyramids are now wholly landscape, Stonehenge but faintly architecture. It follows logically, therefore, that any attempt to arrest this process is to go against the natural order, and that preservation should aim at doing no more than maintaining a building in a state in which it is still capable of being subject to this long transformation. One cannot and should never attempt to put the hands back or even to stop the clock by arbitrarily selecting one stage of this process and crying halt.

Most frequently such attempts are made on the specious plea of 'restoring a building to its original state'. Quite apart from the virtual impossibility of ever achieving this goal, in striving to do so we risk in almost all cases the total destruction of its existing contemporary value. (There is I think one exception to this rule upon which I will touch in a moment.) For architecture is not in the same sense as painting and sculpture a pure art, and therefore alone of the visual arts cannot survive in a museum. Once it fulfils no function save the purely aesthetic, a virtue goes out of it and the sooner it becomes landscape, that is falls into ruin, the better. To illustrate what I mean I can do no better than to cite the case of one of the most celebrated of all the world's buildings. The Church of the Divine Wisdom at Constantinople remained a place of worship for orthodox Christians for over 700 years, and for 500 more as the Mosque of the Prophet fulfilled the same role for the Moslems. Now as Sancta Sophia it is a national monument. Unfortunately, it is only in this last state that I have seen it. To be unimpressed by this stupendous building would be impossible, the beauty of the end is so perfectly matched by the incredible boldness of the means; but one is nevertheless aware, not so much of a disappointment, as of a tiny lack, of which those who knew it in its days as a mosque were never conscious. Someone – in fact the late Ataturk – has cried 'halt' and the natural cycle has been interrupted. For a building such as this can easily withstand a change of function within limits, but not a total suspension of function. One is aware of no such mixed feelings on entering the great Mosque at Nicosia, of infinitely less merit architecturally but still as fine an example of late thirteenth-century French Gothic as you will find outside the Île-de-France, whose bare whitewashed interior is quite empty save for the *mihrab*, the *minbar* and the prayer-rugs beamed on Mecca, and from whose engargoyled towers the muezzin so surprisingly summons. For it is a far, far better thing for the House of God to fall into the hands of the infidel than to pass into the keeping of an Office of Works.

Nor does one feel any sense of disappointment at the total absence of purpose displayed by the Parthenon, for the reward of all good architecture – and even of some bad – of becoming in part landscape has long ago been accorded it. But elsewhere on the Acropolis one does; from the little temple of Nikè Apteros, so carefully, so consciously expertly, put together by the archaeologist there does, for me at least, emerge a faint discouraging whiff of the museum. Just how far one can go in this type of restoration – structurally necessary to some small extent even to preserve ruins as landscape – is a very difficult question to answer. I never saw the Parthenon before the much criticized re-erection of the north colonnade, and I am bound to confess I am conscious of experiencing no lack of intensity, no falling off, on seeing it in its present state. But it does create what I feel to be a dangerous precedent and I am frankly nervous as to what will presently be revealed when the scaffolding comes down from the Propylaea. For ridiculous and idiotic as was Schinkel's proposed scheme for the Acropolis, involving as it did the incorporation of a brand-new palace for King Otho in the current Munich style, I am not altogether certain that, purely in theory, it was not preferable to the dehydrated archaeological approach.

I said, a moment ago, that there was one exception to this ban on total restoration: and it will, I trust, serve to prove the rule. One is only justified in attempting to recreate a building in its original state if these conditions are fulfilled; if one has a truly accurate idea of what its original state, in fact, was; if all continuity between that state and the present has been broken; and if it plays no part in the surrounding landscape. And it is very, very seldom that those three circumstances exist in combination. For example, in the case of the Temple of Nikè, or better still the Treasury of the Athenians at Delphi, thanks to Greek methods of stone-cutting during this period it has been possible to use most of the original stones in their original positions, so that our first condition, save in the matter of colour, is fully met. In addition, thanks to the fact that the very site of Delphi was lost for centuries beneath a mountain village, no sense of continuity is outraged. But, so far from helping the existing landscape, in this case the other ruins, it not only serves to mar it but is itself rendered slightly ridiculous by it. One needs to make not a smaller, but a greater, effort of imagination to relate a building which at first sight in those surroundings looks like a tastefully designed custodian's lodge to one's idea of Delphi as a whole.

On the other hand, such sites as Carcassonne, Caernarvon or Nuremberg fail for different reasons. The available knowledge of their original appearance did not amount to certainty and the imagination of the architect was called in. But not, alas, his creative imagination; only a fumbling, frightened groping for the past. And, moreover, continuity did exist and was disregarded, with the result, particularly at Nuremberg, that one never for a moment felt that the old town bore any relation to the rest of the city, but existed at its heart like the historical section of some international exhibition. How infinitely preferable was Wyatville's treatment of Windsor: its pretensions to genuineness would hardly deceive a four-year-old, but how completely and how soon has it become a part of the landscape in its own right! And this is largely due to the fact that Wyatville has obeyed the instructions which in my youth I so constantly received from my old piano-teacher: 'if you can't be accurate, dear, at least you can strike the wrong note boldly'. Would that all restorers would bear this in mind!

In the case of the Byzantine churches of Ravenna, however, which have recently been elaborately restored, I do feel that our three conditions are in fact fulfilled. Owing to the nature of mosaic, which is of all media the least subject to the ravages of time, and the most easy by modern methods accurately to replace, we are here in no doubt as to the rightness of our conception of the past. As the majority of them are hidden away by modern buildings and all save S. Apollinare in Classe inconspicuous, the landscape, which anyhow in this part of the Adriatic seaboard changes quicker than the architecture, is not affected. But, most important – and in this Ravenna is unique among Italian cities – the continuity of life has been virtually broken. Elsewhere, as at Rome or Florence, most of our pleasure derives from the complete integration of past and present. The poster advertising the charms of Ingrid Bergman or Campari bitters flapping alongside the Renaissance doorway in the Romanesque façade does not distress us, and we accept the abominable Vespas skidding round the base of Michelangelo's David because both are equally, although not equal, manifestations of the Italian genius. But at Ravenna this continuity does not exist; between the city of Theodoric and the modern town there is no link. The monuments of the former are far further removed from present-day Ravenna than the streets of Pompeii from the slums of Naples. So infinitely remote is everything symbolized by the mosaics, so far away does Byzantium seem, that in San Vitale I even resent the presence of the trivial Rococo ceiling painting, whereas elsewhere such traces of the intervening years, the presence of the Baroque wall-tablet above the tortoise stove between the fifteenth-century rood-screen and the Victorian glass, are among the chief sources of my pleasure in old buildings.

Such major problems are not, however, very likely to arise in this country. But on a smaller scale of value they are nowhere more numerous. For we suffer in certain respects from an *embarras de richesses*. Take the question of country houses. In our present circumstances almost every county in England has five times as many fine eighteenth-century examples alone as can possibly be supported in the conditions to which they are accustomed. Apart from the very, very tiny minority which, with or without the aid of the National Trust, can continue to fulfil their original function, how far can their value survive conversion into schools, lunatic asylums or government offices? In so far as their interiors are concerned, hardly at all. Inclusion in a museum may be the kiss of death, but it is only a death of the spirit. Conversion into a reform school means physical annihilation as well. They must depend, therefore, for their survival upon the merits of their exteriors and their value in the landscape. So long as these can be preserved, do what you will with the interiors; if they cannot, remove the roof and let them fall into ruin.

In this connection I have at last one practical suggestion, for even in a talk so avowedly theoretical as this one should allow one's feet to touch the ground just once. Far too often in striving to save the whole we lose the chance of preserving the most valuable part, the façade. A chain-store, let us say, buys a corner site in a market town occupied by a pleasant eighteenth-century brick building, not particularly distinguished in itself but playing a vital role in the general effect of the market square. A few enthusiasts, knowing only too well the feast of chromium and black glass which is shortly to be theirs, start an agitation and finally persuade the local authority to issue a preservation order. Two years pass during which the purchasers do nothing with their property, windows get broken, rain and decay set in. They then return to the charge, pleading that the premises are now utterly incapable of any sort of conversion short of a total demolition, and this time with the support of the local councillors who feel that the derelict at the town's centre is bad for trade, win their case. Now, if at the beginning a preservation order had been issued for the façade alone, agreement could probably have been reached.

An admirable example of this type of preservation is provided by Crewe House, the value of which for the passer-by has actually been increased by the clearing away of the old wall in front. And it is, one understands, the principle to be adopted in the case of Carlton House Terrace. Let it be far more generally applied, and let us have no cavilling from the purists who would condemn such practices as architectural falsehood and a betrayal of functional principles. For the most important function of such façades, that of focusing and maintaining an existing landscape, is being fulfilled, and who can doubt that this is of considerably greater value than the activities of the civil servants, or fancy-goods importers or mentally defective children, which are being carried on, at perhaps some infinitesimal loss of convenience, behind them. Business-men may grumble that the expense of such conversions is sometimes greater than rebuilding. No matter; that is a little sacrifice they should be prepared to make for the sake of the community even if – which is most unlikely – it costs them as much as a tenth of what they annually spend on what is so curiously known as 'prestige advertising'.

Some of you may think that all I have said is very fine, but ultimately irrelevant. That the backward glance is not only unnecessary but positively dangerous. That a preoccupation with the past, while understandable enough in the case of those who have not got one, such as the Americans, is a foolishness which less reactionary, more forward-looking people should eschew. Aligning yourselves in fact with the late lamented Signor Marinetti, and repeating, albeit perhaps unconsciously, the sentiments so powerfully expressed in the Futurist Manifesto, you cry for a clean slate.

Let me remind you that, no matter how contemporary you strive to be, scratch as a starting-point is forever unattainable. That whereas it remains questionable whether we do mount on our dead selves to higher things, it is certain that we can get nowhere if we reject the assistance afforded by other people. Without the continuous deposits of architectural humus no modern architecture can thrive, and if we scrape away the topsoil it will inevitably wither away. For no matter how clearly we envisage our objectives, no one can build the New Jerusalem in a spiritual dust-bowl.

'*That's St Paul's, that was!*'

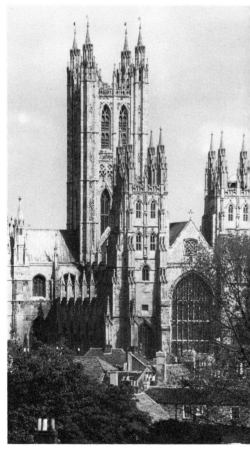

*Canterbury Cathedral from the west, before and after the destruction of the N.W. tower and George Austin's replacement in 1834*

# V    A restoration tragedy: cathedrals in the eighteenth and nineteenth centuries

ONE OF the ironies of the Gothic Revival is that it largely destroyed the very buildings from which it drew its inspiration. Considerably more medieval architecture was lost through restoration than through demolition. Why did the architects of the medieval movement show so little understanding for medieval buildings? The answer is surely twofold: over-zealousness and over-confidence. Scott and his generation were sincerely motivated by religious devotion; spurred on by the Ecclesiological Society, they saw it as their mission to rebuild churches that were ruinous through years of neglect, and to make them fit for the service of God. Also, the prosperity and confidence of the nineteenth century, which inspired the great building programme of the Gothic Revival, was accompanied, as in most periods of intense architectural activity, by a lack of respect for existing buildings. The decayed state of the fabric of many cathedrals offended Scott and his colleagues, and led them to reface and recarve true Gothic, in a deliberate attempt to make it conform to the smooth finish and crisp outlines to which they had become accustomed, in their own churches. And aesthetically they disliked the mixture of styles that characterized most cathedrals. Confident that they had mastered Gothic just as capably as any medieval mason, they set themselves to correct the inconsistencies. Without, in their own eyes, compromising their respect for the originals, they were, nevertheless, convinced that their own buildings were better.

One can understand the lack of sympathy shown by Wren, Essex or even Wyatt for medieval buildings, which to them appeared old-fashioned and crude. But for the Gothicists to treat with such a lack of comprehension the very buildings that they devoted their lives to emulating was particularly culpable. It was as though Smirke or Wilkins had decided to rebuild the Parthenon with improvements. Holman Hunt looking back at this dilemma, in 1904, said: 'No individual could hope to stay the destruction that false taste and jobbery were effecting throughout the Empire. It must be understood that the greatest destroyers of artistic beauty and architectural history were not their declared enemies. . . . The great destroyers were . . . the resurrectionists of Gothic

Salisbury Cathedral, Beauchamp Chapel,
demolished by Wyatt, 1789

Hereford, the west front before the fall of the
west tower

in what was called the "correct period".'[1] And William Morris summed
up the situation in the following words, as true today as when they were
written:

These old buildings have been altered and added to century after century,
often beautifully – always historically; their value lay in that; they have suffered almost always from neglect; also, often, from violence, but ordinary . . .
mending would almost always have kept them standing; pieces of nature and
of history.

But of late years a great uprising of ecclesiastical zeal, coinciding with a
great increase of study, and consequently of knowledge of medieval
architecture, has driven people into spending their money on these buildings,
not merely with the purpose of repairing them, of keeping them safe, clean,
and wind- and watertight, but also of restoring them to some ideal state of
perfection; sweeping away, if possible, all signs of what has befallen them, at
least since the Reformation, and often dates much earlier.

This has sometimes been done with much disregard of art, and entirely
from ecclesiastical zeal, but oftener it has been well meant enough as regards
art.[2]

Many of the restoration theories which men like Scott later developed,
had been formulated by James Wyatt more than fifty years earlier. One
might have expected Wyatt, after his own excursions into Gothic at
Fonthill, to have shown more sympathy for medieval Gothic than he in
fact demonstrated. His appallingly harsh treatment of nearly all the
cathedrals in his care, despite the rage and despair of John Carter, Pugin,
Ruskin and the Society of Antiquaries, set a precedent for Scott, and the
true Gothicists who followed. Sometimes, as at Salisbury, his passion
for uniformity led him to remove all later additions. Horace Walpole

*Hereford, the west front after restoration, 1788 onwards*

*Hereford, the west front as rebuilt by Oldrid Scott, 1904*

wrote in 1789 of Wyatt's demolition of the Beauchamp and Hungerford chapels: 'I shall heartily lament with you, Sir, the demolition of those beautiful chapels at Salisbury. I was scandalized long ago at the ruinous state in which they were indecently suffered to remain. It appears strange that when a spirit of restoration and decoration has taken place, it should be mixed with such barbarous invention.'[3]

That 'barbarous invention' was given full rein at Hereford, where, after the fall of the west tower, Wyatt created a new west front, but in the process destroyed the Norman triforium and clerestory, and rebuilt them 'in a style imitated from the Early English at Salisbury',[4] where he had just been working – hardly an appropriate style for a Norman cathedral. He also removed the spire from the central tower. In 1867 an anonymous article accused Wyatt at Hereford of '"Brummagem" performances [which] have been the great trouble of succeeding architects. [He] received £13,000 for his pains, and declared it to be the cheapest job he had ever done in his life.'[5]

'Following the same destructive course as at Salisbury', he also 'removed many monuments from their original positions, thereby rendering even their identification a matter of some difficulty. . . . With Wyatt, restoration meant destruction.'[6]

Pugin visited Hereford in 1833.

I rushed to the cathedral; but horror! dismay! the villain Wyatt had been there, the west front was his. Need I say more? No! All that is vile, cunning and rascally is included in the term Wyatt, and I could hardly summon sufficient fortitude to enter and examine the interior. In this church there is much to admire, a good deal to learn, and much to deplore. . . . Only conceive the fine Saxon [i.e. Norman] ornaments imitated in plaster in the most wretched style; a plain ceiling to the nave; the Lady Chapel filled with bookcases, and the end towards the church plastered up.[7]

Pugin was equally incensed by Wyatt's alterations at Lichfield:

... its distant appearance promised great things, what was my horror and astonishment on perceiving the west front to have been restored with brown cement, cracked in every direction, with heads worked on with the trowel, devoid of all expression or feeling, crockets as bad, and a mixture of all styles. My surprise, however, ceased on the verger's informing me that the whole church was improved and beautified about thirty years ago by the late Mr Wyatt. Yes, this monster of architectural depravity – this pest of cathedral architecture – has been here.[8]

Wyatt's treatment of Durham shows no greater sensitivity. The proposal to remove the superb Galilee Chapel was defeated by the Society of Antiquaries, as was his attempt to destroy the beautiful fourteenth-century stone reredos. But they were too late to save the chapter house. Sir Harry Englefield, Vice-President of the Society of Antiquaries reported:

The apse of the chapter house and parts of its north and south walls were levelled to the ground; its vaulted ceiling and its ancient pavement were destroyed. A new chapter house had been built, with sash windows, stuccoed walls with a neat cornice, marble chimney pieces, and curtains, a mahogany table with a satin-wood border, and mahogany chairs with horse-hair seats.[9]

Wyatt had turned a Norman chapter house into a Georgian drawing room.

At Westminster Abbey, where Wyatt was appointed Surveyor to the Fabric in 1776, his principal contribution was the refacing and re-decoration of the exterior of the Henry VII Chapel, work that William Morris condemned for 'taking all the romance out of . . . the most romantic work of the late middle ages'.[10] The chapel was, however, in a lamentable condition, and Wyatt's repair, although extremely thorough, seems to have been largely accurate. 'The renovation of the external architecture has been completed and with the exception of the ornamental parts of the upper battlements . . . all the ancient work has been correctly imitated . . . as nearly as possible, in exact conformity to the original building,'[11] said Neale in 1818.

To Wyatt, however, we owe the landscaping of cathedral closes. Although, at Salisbury, this involved the demolition of the beautiful thirteenth-century bell tower, it created perhaps the finest setting for a cathedral in England. By removing the medieval jumble of buildings and broken tombstones which had previously surrounded it, and treating the cathedral like a great eighteenth-century house in a landscape park, he provided the opportunity for it to be seen in the round, which is denied to most French cathedrals.

*Rochester: Cottingham's drawing as it was before 1825; his design for a new tower; and Hodgson-Fowler's restoration of 1904*

The early nineteenth century saw several examples of stylistic barbarism. At Rochester, in 1825, L. N. Cottingham demolished the central tower and spire, and rebuilt it in plain Gothic without a spire. It remained thus for eighty years until C. Hodgson-Fowler disposed of Cottingham's work and constructed a new tower and spire, roughly based on seventeenth-century prints. His son, N. J. Cottingham, 'who rebuilt rather than restored, and allowed his workmen to re-work ancient sculptures',[12] followed Wyatt at Hereford. (The Dean and Chapter had previously consulted William Burges as to Cottingham's fitness for the job. It is a tragedy that he, and not Burges, was employed.) He demolished all the post-Norman additions to the cracked central piers and made them good; removed the pulpitum; rebuilt the east end of the chancel, removing the Perpendicular window and replacing it by three broad lancets; and carried out a drastic restoration of the Lady Chapel.

At Canterbury George Austin, in 1834, removed the Norman north-west tower, slightly ruinous, and replaced it with a copy of the existing south-west tower. Symmetry was gained, at the expense of Lanfranc's fine tower.

Perkins, at Worcester, 'altered all the windows',[13] and drastically restored the building. He replaced a fine late eighteenth-century east window by Early English lancets. The *Builder* condemned these, not quite fairly, 'as poor in design, as meagre and ineffective in moulding, and as coarse in execution as can be conceived; almost as bad as the one remaining in the west front'; this was replaced by Scott.[14]

Besides Scott, the other architects chiefly responsible for cathedral restoration during the nineteenth century were Blore, Salvin, Street, Burges, Jackson, Pearson and Blomfield.

Sir George Gilbert Scott was the most prolific of them and his name crops up again and again in any account of the restoration of our churches and cathedrals. As he had an undue share of commissions he has received, perhaps, an undue share of blame. One should in fairness remember the conditions in which he worked. He had to carry out the instructions of his clients, the Deans and Chapters, who wished to move with the times, and to whose arguments he was naturally susceptible. Diocesan authorities are as culpable as the architects they employ, and, where cathedrals are concerned, they still (unhappily) exert total control. Scott himself was aware of this dilemma at St Albans where he said: 'I am in this, as in other works, obliged to face right and left to combat at once two enemies from either hand, one wanting me to do too much, and the other finding fault with me for doing anything at all.'[15] (Scott attempted to curb the zeal of the Restoration Committee, whereas Lord Grimthorpe, after Scott's death, having virtually bought St Alban's Abbey, was able to lead the Committee by the nose.)

The preservationists, the second enemy to whom Scott referred, only appeared in force towards the end of his life – and had little influence upon him, although it was as a protest against his restorations that the Society for the Protection of Ancient Buildings was founded.

Scott's historical knowledge was a dominating factor, both in his own architecture, and in his restorations. His accounts of his patient researches, by which he gradually pieced together the clues, read at times like a detective novel. The excitement with which he sifted the evidence, and the accuracy of some of his reconstructions, show the extent of his own archaeological knowledge, without which these rescue operations would not have been possible.

On the other hand moral zeal and professional ambition frequently outran his better judgment. His restorations fall into two categories; those carried out under the influence of the Ecclesiologists, when he deliberately altered buildings to the 'ideal' Middle Pointed thirteenth-century Gothic, and those dominated by his own historical sense, in which he reinstated 'original' features. Both could be equally destructive. His creative furnishings, to which I shall refer later, were dictated by liturgical requirements.

He says himself: 'we have completely revolutionized our ecclesiastical architecture. . . . The base architecture of the churches of thirty years back is overthrown, and the noble style of our medieval forefathers re-established on its ruins.'[16] Unfortunately, this noble thirteenth-century style was re-established at the expense of much irreplaceable fabric of earlier periods, and for this Scott cannot be forgiven. When an architect decides to replace genuine Gothic by Gothic of his own contriving, confidence has overreached itself.

At Ely, one of his earlier commissions, the quality of Scott's work is excellent and, especially in the rebuilding of the octagon, shows his aptitude for archaeological research at its best. This had been rebuilt in 1757 by James Essex, making it smaller and less impressive. Scott removed Essex's incorrect octagon, and reinstated its original form, based on Browne-Willis's engravings: 'The design of the central lantern I most carefully investigated from ancient evidences, and can speak of it with great certainty. The great evidences were the mortices and the carpenter's marks.'[17] Scott's beautiful drawings are now safely in the Victoria and Albert Museum. (Many similar drawings in cathedral archives and local record offices suffer from neglect; their historical value still remains unrecognized.)

Scott reinstated the upper octagon windows (altered by Essex) and embellished the diagonal sides of the lower octagon with statues of the Apostles by Redfern. Gambier Parry's painting of the lantern was criticized by the *Builder* in 1875: 'There were little or no visible precedents for colouring found to guide the present work when the woodwork . . . was cleared of whitewash. Some remnants of red or blue were found, but exhibiting no principles of artistic arrangement. There was no ornamental coloured design anywhere.'[18] However, the Clerk of Works stated that: 'sufficient remains of the ancient painting were discovered . . . to serve as a guide for a safe restoration of the patterns and colouring; the restoration of this painting would greatly add to the magnificence and beauty of the cathedral'.[19] On this occasion one must agree that whatever its authenticity, some decoration was justified, though the paintings of angels inside the upper octagon cannot honestly be admired.

The open timber roof of the nave had been considered unsatisfactory for years; in 1771, James Bentham complained of the lack of a 'proper ceiling'.[20] The original horizontal wooden ceiling, if it existed, would probably have resembled that of Peterborough, but had been replaced by a high-pitched roof; this remained unceiled and undecorated until, as Scott recorded, 'under my suggestion, and with my co-operation, the ceiling . . . was [constructed and] painted by Mr Le Strange and Mr Gambier Parry. I suggested . . . the ceiling of St Michael's Hildesheim as a model.'[21] (Had this idea been prompted by a paper given before the Cambridge Architectural Society by the Rev. Mr Williams in 1858 – 'Ecclesiological Notes on Hildesheim'?) Le Strange 'spared no labour in the examination of manuscript authorities for ornamentation. . . . The general design was cast upon the model of the Jesse tree.'[22] The decorative scheme which evolved provides us with one of the finest ceilings of any period, and an authentic re-creation of Norman decoration. Of his ceiling in the west tower, representing God in the act of creating the Universe, with the inscription 'I am before all things and by all things exist,' Scott says: 'The style of decoration is that which prevailed in England about the close of the 12th century, when this part of the tower was completed.'[23] This work is artistically and archaeologically a *tour de force*.

However, having painted the nave and west tower ceilings, Scott

St Albans, central tower

The shrine of St Alban, as restored by
Scott, 1873

felt that the uncoloured state of the walls and arches of the naves produced a coldness and 'raw light', and 'determined to proceed with the
colouring of the walls as soon as possible'.[24] The work was fortunately
never carried out. The Victorians always found it hard to judge when
they had had enough of a good thing. Scott also reinstated Norman
windows in the south aisle, in the place of later ones: a very quesionable
alteration. Ely is one of the few cathedrals in which he retained part of
the original marble pavement of the choir, which he here 'combined
with Minton tiles' – the first occasion on which he had used these in a
cathedral.[25] He also conceived, and Skidmore made, the first of his
magnificent open screens here (the main screen is of wood, those of the
choir aisles metal); many of his other furnishings (such as the gaseliers)
were of high quality.

Of his work at St Albans, Scott wrote in 1871: 'No church in Britain
more thoroughly deserves a more careful and conservative restoration,
nor would any more richly repay his labour of love' – an ironic comment
in view of Lord Grimthorpe's subsequent iniquities.[26]

Scott was called in, in 1870, after the discovery of a crushed pier under
the central tower, which was found to have been deliberately pierced at
an earlier period. He immediately set a team of workmen to shore up
the tower, and for weeks they worked, on twenty-four-hour shifts,
amidst the roar of falling rubble and of cracking masonry.[27] This
preserved the tower, which remains one of the few authentic parts of the
Abbey; gratitude is due to Scott for the speed and restraint with which
he acted.

*Chichester, ruins left by collapse of the central tower in 1861, and the cathedral today with central tower rebuilt by Scott and N.W. tower by Pearson, 1901*

A contemporary account of Scott's discovery and re-erection of St Alban's shrine also shows his respect for the past:

Sir Gilbert Scott, in the course of restoration of the Abbey, ordered the walling up of the east end of the south aisle to be removed, February 1872, when behind it was found an immense quantity of carved fragments of stone. . . . The search was diligently prosecuted, the remaining western arches of the Lady Chapel were opened, the gabled panels of the ends and side arcades were found, and at length the marble work of the shrine was almost perfectly recovered. But it was in hundreds of little fragments. . . . The fragments were, however, found in such regular order that they almost explained their place in the design. As soon as the general plan was made out, the work of rebuilding was commenced, a work of enormous difficulty . . . continued with laborious patience and ingenuity till the whole was put together . . . in a more perfect condition than even the more famous shrine of St Edward at Westminster . . .[28]

Praise is long overdue for Scott's many conservative repairs, and resourceful salvage operations, without which some of our cathedrals might no longer be there today. He undoubtedly saved the central tower of St Albans from collapse. He would almost certainly have saved that of Chichester, which fell through the incompetence of Slater, who, oblivious to the danger, was busy refurnishing the choir when the tower fell. Scott was only called in after its collapse. His rebuilding, to the original design, using many of the original stones, was a masterly piece of thoughtful reconstruction.

He might also have obviated Pearson's controversial rebuilding of the central tower at Peterborough, had his urgent recommendations been carried out when they were made. The Dean and Chapter, having failed to act on Scott's advice, paid for their procrastination; for, by the time the condition of the tower had become critical, and Pearson was called in by telegram, complete rebuilding was thought necessary.

In 1860 Scott said of Peterborough:

A few years back my attention had been called to . . . increasing subsidence all along the north side of the church . . . of an alarming character. I strongly advised that the north aisle of the nave should be securely shored up and this was done, but for a very long time the Chapter . . . did all in their power to shut their own eyes, and those of the public to the truth. . . . The central tower, which had been affected by the general movement northwards . . . is in a very sad state, and nothing is doing. Some of the Chapter, when their eyes were unwillingly opened, wanted to go beyond me, and to have flying buttresses built against the north aisle wall. I do not like this, because it would so seriously affect its aspect.[29]

Scott's account of his discovery and re-creation of the chapter house at Westminster also reveals the excitement that dominated much nineteenth-century restoration.

Seldom do we see a noble work of art reduced to such a wreck! It appears that, as early as the days of Edward III (certainly before 1340), it was made over, I suppose occasionally, to the use of the House of Commons, on condition that it should be kept in repair by the Crown. In or after the reign of Edward VI, however, St Stephen's Chapel being given up to the House of Commons, the chapter house was converted into a Public Record Office. In or about 1740, the vaulting was found to be dangerous, and taken down; and before this, in 1703, we find that Sir Christopher Wren having refused to put up a gallery in it, it was made over to the tender mercies of some barbarian, who fitted it up for the records, with studious regard to concealment or destruction of its architectural beauties.

I undertook some years back, the careful investigation of its details, and such was the difficulty presented by the fittings and other impediments, that, though every possible facility was afforded me by the gentlemen in charge of the records, it occupied me (on and off) for several months.

I believe, however, that I succeeded in getting at nearly every part of the design. . . .

. . . The windows are almost entirely walled up, though a considerable part of the tracery, no doubt, remains embedded. Their design is, however, readily ascertainable, one of them being a blank, owing to one face of the octagon being in contact with the transept of the church: a nobler four-light window could hardly be found.

The window over the doorway is most carefully walled up with ashlar, but from the bases visible on its sill, we see that it was of five instead of four lights – no doubt to avoid the stumped look it might have had from being so much shortened by the height of the doorway and the abutting vestibule. I had often wondered that, while the windows generally are walled up with *brick*, this should be filled with *stone*; but on taking out one of the ashlar stones

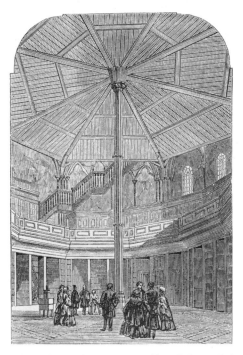

*Chapter house of Westminster Abbey, before and after restoration by Scott in 1865*

to ascertain the section of the jamb, what was my surprise at finding them to consist entirely of the lengths of moulded ribs of the lost vaulting, carefully packed, like wine-bottles in a bin, with their moulded sides inwards! I made a still more interesting discovery in the spandrels of the doorway below. The gallery crosses the head of this doorway, and the presses for records were fitted so closely to the wall that nothing could be seen. I was one day on the top of one of these presses, and on venturing to pull away an arris fillet which closed the crevice between it and the wall, I perceived the top of an arched recess in the wall behind the press and on looking down into it I saw some round object of stone in the recess below. My curiosity being excited, I let down into it by a string a small bull's-eye lantern, when, to my extreme delight, I saw that the mysterious object in hand was the head of a beautiful full-sized statue in a niche. Permission was speedily obtained for the removal of the press. The statue proved to be a very fine one of the Virgin, and in the spaces adjoining were angels censing. I afterwards found that it formed part of an Annunciation; the angel having been on the other side of the door. This last-named figure has, however, been long since moved into the vestibule. Its wings are gone; but the mortices into which they were fixed remain. Both are fine works, though not devoid of a remnant of Byzantine stiffness.[30]

So much for Scott's detective work. Although his treatment of the chapter house was carried out with the approval of the Society of Antiquaries, the comments of William Burges, one of Scott's most notable contemporaries, are interesting: 'We dread any attempt at

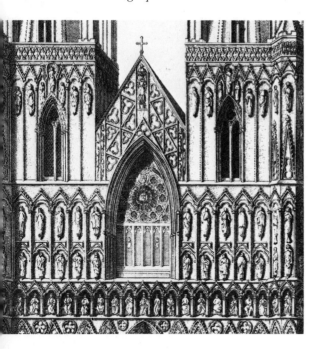

*Lichfield Cathedral, detail of west front before Scott's restoration*

*Lichfield Cathedral: Scott's first design for the west window and (right) after restoration*

restoration lest damage should be done to its precious fragments, any attempt to make a smart new building will be worse than leaving the place alone.' These remarks show his critical reaction to the thorough restorations of the period, despite his Ecclesiological sympathies. He also said: 'It is to be hoped that there will be no hurry in deciding the execution of the stained glass; the state of this manufacture – for at present it is no more – is not such as to warrant haste. As there is *so much valuable wall-painting* there can scarcely be any doubt that much of this *glass should be grisaille* so as not to exclude the light.'[31] Burges's comments on the state of stained-glass manufacture are interesting – in view of his own use of Burne-Jones glass for Waltham Abbey. The request for grisaille fell on deaf ears. Scott's solution is familiar to all.

His own commitment to thirteenth-century Gothic, however, inevitably affected his respect for architecture of other periods.

In his report for the Dean and Chapter on the west front of Rochester Cathedral he said: 'The Norman remains . . . are almost too valuable to be interfered with. It is . . . an open question whether a restoration, in part conjectural, should be attempted, or whether it may not be best to adhere to the present form of the front, and to limit our operations to mere necessary repairs.'[32] This was an unusual concession for Scott. He died before many of his recommendations at Rochester could be carried out, and it fell to Pearson to reface and reconstruct parts of the west front.

Scott lived, however, to see his remodelling of the east end of Rochester completed. Of this he says: 'It owes its main disfigurement

to an earlier date. Its upper range of windows were taken out in the fifteenth or sixteenth century, and a very uncouth window substituted; this seems as if it had been removed a century later, and again in our own day [by Cottingham]. I feel that it ought to be restored to its original form which is ascertainable . . . from remnants still existing. The lower windows of the east end were', Scott suggests, 'fitted with fourteenth-century tracery, which has been renewed in our own day [Cottingham again]. Had it been the actual tracery added in the fourteenth century, I should have been favourable to its retention; but, being only a modern copy . . . it should give way to the integrity of the Early English design.'[33] And so it did. But Scott's east end was an improvement on Cottingham's, and more in character with the building.

As part of the 'authenticating' of the west front of Lichfield, he entirely rebuilt the old west window, from a design of his own but based on Hollar's prints. He called the existing window 'debased', and boasted of replacing it with 'a more ecclesiologically satisfying design'.[34] Similarly, at Worcester, which had already received harsh stylistic treatment from Perkins, Scott redesigned the west window, and much of the dull west front, extensively altered the fine tower and marred the north porch with horrible statues commissioned from Boulton. His re-casing of the exterior of both Lichfield and Worcester very largely destroyed their historical value. An appeal is now under way for the replacement of much of Scott's stonework at Worcester, again in a decayed condition.

His alterations to the exterior of the choir and Lady Chapel at Hereford

*Oxford Cathedral before and after Scott's rebuilding of the east end, 1853*

were also insensitive; but his most drastic remodelling took place at
Chester, where he transformed an authentic medieval building into one
that could almost be mistaken for one of his own Gothic Revival
churches. Externally, in addition to the usual refacing, Scott's inter-
ferences included the ugly turrets of the central tower, the ridiculously
over-sized turrets with spires, flanking the east end, and the inept spired
chapel at the east end of the south choir aisle. His handsome roof in the
nave to some extent redeems his work, but his deliberate re-styling of the
east end, and his replacement of the existing Perpendicular windows
with Early English lancets was inexcusably arrogant. At Oxford
Cathedral also, he destroyed a fine fourteenth-century east window,
and replaced it with his own late Norman wheel window, thus completely altering the character of the building.

Westminster Abbey was, for Scott, the ideal on which he based so
many of his own buildings. His attitudes here are therefore especially
revealing; and what they reveal is, above all, lack of sensitivity.

His remodelling of the magnificent north transept front (completed
by J. L. Pearson) was one of his most notorious pieces of architectural
vandalism. Scott criticized Wren, who had previously repaired the
portal, for having 'wretchedly tampered' with it; but he himself finally
destroyed its medieval appearance altogether, in a deliberate attempt to

*The north transept of Westminster Abbey in 1654, before restoration by Wren; (above right) in about 1880, in course of alteration; and today, showing later changes by Scott and Pearson*

return the porch to its original, 'ideal' state. His alterations were intended as improvements, for, he says: 'these magnificent portals (north and west), formed . . . the most sumptuous external features in the Church . . . and must have been gorgeously rich'.[35] In his attempt to return to this 'sumptuous' original, Scott destroyed not only much medieval stonework, but also all traces of Wren's existing facing with its semi-classical detailing.

He cheerfully admitted the lack of evidence for his own restoration:

Of the original details . . . it is nearly impossible to form anything like a correct idea. The whole was greatly decayed at the commencement of the last century, and was recased, almost throughout, with Oxfordshire stone, by Sir Christopher Wren and his successors, the details being altered and pared down in a very merciless manner; and the work, thus renewed, has again become greatly decayed. There is, in fact, scarcely a trace of original detail of the eastern portion of the exterior left.[36]

Scott's systematic recasing, however, was itself largely abortive, because, by 1884, when further refacing was proposed, the Society for the Protection of Ancient Buildings reported:

Upon careful examination it was found that some of the worst parts were those which had been refaced from time to time. Where the original Godstone facing remains untouched . . . the walling is sound; whereas, where the walls have been refaced, not only has the substance of the walling been shaken, but the facing itself is decayed. It is a continual marvel to this Society, how lightly the so-called guardians of our beautiful medieval buildings, and their professional advisers, enter upon the serious work of renewing what cannot be renewed without fears of irreparable injury. In dealing with such a building as West-minster Abbey – each original stone should be numbered and dealt with as a precious jewel.[37]

Scott's failure to use suitable stone is surprising in view of his sardonic comment that 'the stone, brought from Yorkshire, for the Palace of Westminster, seems likely to perish in thirty [years], and this after the country had been at great expense in making inquiries and experiments by the most scientific men of the day'.[38] However, he made the same mistake himself, over Wakefield Bridge Chapel where his strong commercial sense overcame his artistic sensibility. He devoted himself 'with the greatest earnestness to the investigation of the relics of the destroyed detail' of a fifteenth-century chapel, and

made, I believe, a very perfect design. The work . . . would have been a great success, but that the contractor . . . had a handsome offer made him for the semi-decayed front, to set up in a park nearby. He them made an offer to execute a new front in place of the weather beaten old one . . . and his offer was accepted. . . . I am filled with wonder how I ever was induced to consent to it . . . as it was contrary to the principles of my own report. . . . The new front was a perfect masterpiece of beautiful workmanship, but it was *new*, and in just retribution the Caen stone is now [1864] more rotten than the old work, which is set up in some gentleman's grounds [Kettlethorpe Hall]. I think of this with the utmost shame and chagrin.[39]

Scott, although repentant in retrospect, never seemed to learn. Much of the arbitrary quality of his work can be blamed upon his commercial ambition. He was an excellent businessman, and seldom turned down a commission, with the result that many of his restorations were insufficiently supervised. At Salisbury, the repainting of the Lady Chapel was carried out while he was laid up, and was 'not faithfully reproduced from the old remains', while he only visited St Albans three times during his extensive restoration.

Scott's structural alterations were, as we have seen, often drastic enough, but it was above all his re-working of the stone that gave the cathedrals which he restored their distinctive appearance. Lichfield, Hereford, Worcester, Chester and several others no longer retain an appearance of antiquity. Many of the original features and the splendour of the overall design remain, but the finish is unmistakably Victorian. In achieving an overall unanimity of texture, the medieval quality has been obliterated. The position taken up by the Society for the Protection of Ancient Buildings was, on occasion, as extreme as that of Scott. Neither total replacement nor total retention of damaged stonework is desirable. The complete inactivity proposed by the Society for the Protection of Ancient Buildings over the repair of the hopelessly decayed tracery of the window bays of the cloisters at Canterbury was quite impractical; whereas Scott's drastic restoration of the cloisters at Westminster and Salisbury was destructive to their character.

Of the other principal Gothic Revival architects involved in restoration William Burges was the most outstanding for his imaginative approach to old buildings. His aim was to do for architecture what the Pre-Raphaelites had done for painting. By this he meant not the re-creation of a lifeless copy, but the creation of a living work of art, based on a deep understanding and respect for the style and techniques of the medieval builders.

Burges, unlike Scott, possessed exceptional originality, and also, unlike Scott, a profound sensitivity towards medieval architecture. This led him to a recognition that a cathedral or a parish church could not be regarded as a vehicle for self-expression at the expense of its original character. He said however: 'A great cathedral is an encyclopaedia of all the knowledge of the time. It is only by acting in the same way that we shall ever have an art of our own.'[40] By this he implied that any legitimate additions must be carried out in the spirit of the medieval craftsman. Burges' contempt for Scott's methods is clearly shown in his report on the Westminster chapter house, already quoted. This contempt for the copyist was shared later by Norman Shaw, and frequently used unfairly to condemn the whole Gothic Revival movement.

His restoration of Waltham Abbey was a successful vindication of these words. His repair of the stonework was extremely conservative, and he inserted windows of his own design only into the east end of the truncated nave, where none had existed. In order to proclaim his faith in craftsmanship, he commissioned, in 1861, one of Burne-Jones' finest stained-glass windows. Unfortunately, the same praise cannot be given to his proposals for the decoration of St Paul's Cathedral, with which he was out of sympathy. He would have liked to see much of the classical decoration chiselled off, and an attempt made to provide a medieval scheme of decoration for the interior. Fortunately, his designs, like so many others, were rejected.[41]

Burges proved successfully that medievalism could be applied to domestic buildings as well as to churches, and his commissions for the Marquis of Bute are a convincing re-creation of medieval ideas expressed in modern terms.

Blore, an architect with a flourishing country house practice, was, rather surprisingly since he had little ecclesiastical experience, commissioned to work on the restoration of the choir at Peterborough and on the west front of Norwich, and was subsequently appointed as surveyor to Westminster Abbey. Blore's new altar, choir screen and stalls at Peterborough were completed in 1831, and were much admired. However, by 1862, they were out of favour: 'design and colour are alike unpleasing, but allowance should be made for the period when the work was done.'[42] They were all swept away by Pearson in 1883.

At Westminster Abbey, Blore designed the present admirable choir stalls, and the west front of the choir screen. His stalls, an early essay in nineteenth-century Gothic, blend successfully with the earlier work, and are worthy of their prominent position. However, Blore also, according to Lethaby, 'struck at the lovely early fourteenth-century bays of the cloister, and put new in their place, and gave the north front of the nave another dressing',[43] to its detriment. The cloister was later restored by Scott, and has just emerged from another major repair.

Lethaby, however, had the last word on the Westminster controversy:

How different it would have been with Westminster if instead of theory learning and caprice, this energy in pulling down and setting up – if, instead of all this, there had been steadily carried on during the last century a system of patching, staying and repairs, – a sort of building dentistry. Even yet if we could arrest the process of so-called improvements which is slowly creeping over the whole building in a sort of deadly paralysis, and substitute more daily carefulness, much might be handed on for other ages.[44]

Anthony Salvin was an architect chiefly distinguished for his scholarly castle restorations and for his thriving country house practice. His extensive restoration to the Norman fabric of both Norwich and Durham cathedrals is less well documented. At Norwich he remodelled the choir and installed a new organ. He redesigned the pulpitum: 'The

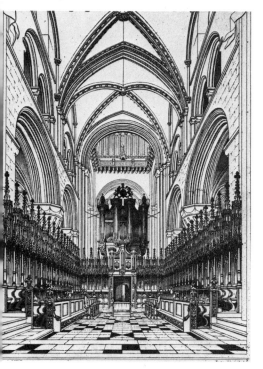

*The choir of Durham Cathedral, looking west, before Salvin's restoration and after Scott's*

lower part, which is ancient, has been restored. . . . The upper part, which was completed in 1833, is heavy and ugly, and its effect is by no means improved by the decoration above it,'[45] said a report of 1862. (It has now been cut down and simplified.) He also partially rebuilt the south transept and refaced it in Bath stone.

At Durham, to the consternation of the *Gentleman's Magazine*,[46] Salvin opened up the choir, removing Bishop Cosin's superb seventeenth-century Baroque choir screen and stalls, with Bishop Crewe's organ above. The stalls were pushed back between the great Norman piers, thus halving their number and making them invisible from the nave. (Scott brought them out again to their proper position in front of the piers.) Salvin also replaced Cosin's magnificent font and canopy (now fortunately reinstated) by a huge Norman font of his own, and removed all the decorative woodwork surrounding St Cuthbert's tomb. His sortie into the field of cathedral restoration was thus not without its disasters.

The work of George Edmund Street bore the hallmark of his master, Scott, in whose office he trained, and of the Ecclesiological Society. He built in robust thirteenth-century Gothic, magnificently detailed and executed, but deliberately confined within a very narrow stylistic range, arguing that by confining himself to one style and one period the architect could avoid becoming eclectic or imitative. He boasted of being a medievalist, and denied that this 'implies a desire to refuse this age what its history entitles it to demand. We . . . wish to do our work in the same simple but strong spirit which made the man of the thirteenth century so noble a creature . . . in the same sense . . . as the Pre-Raphaelites have taken their name . . . [as] a pledge of resistance to false and modern systems of thought and practice in art'.[47]

Street successfully applied these theories to his own churches, which are a reflection of his words: 'in stonework and the science of moulding; in sculpture of figure and foliage; in metalwork, iron or silver . . . and stained glass, the northern art of the thirteenth century is pure, vigorous and . . . true',[48] but at York Minster, where he rebuilt the clerestory and refaced the south transept front, adding new gables and pinnacles, his work is more suspect. At Bristol, Street succeeded Scott, who had already proposed the reconstruction of the nave, and in his report to the Dean and Chapter also recommended the removal of the magnificent stone pulpitum of 1542 to give more space – 'The primary demand is for a nave of the greatest possible capacity'.[49] Perhaps he hoped to get the job himself.

Some of Scott's proposals, including the vandalistic removal of the pulpitum, were carried out disastrously by T. E. Pope in 1858. His sanctuary was criticized by the *Ecclesiologist*: 'the pattern and materials are such as would disgrace a railway station, or the showroom of a cheap lath and plaster warehouse'. Pope's new stone screen, with no sides, gave the choir the appearance of 'the gate to a field with the hedges taken away. The screen is an absurd waste of money and of no use whatsoever'.[50] It was later replaced by Pearson's elaborate and beautiful existing screen.

It fell to Street, however, to rebuild the nave; the site had been used, since the Reformation, for a variety of uses, and some attempt at reconstruction had been made earlier in the nineteenth century. Street removed the fifteenth-century north walk of the cloister, which had been extended over the position of the original fourteenth-century nave; cleared the site; and re-erected the remains of the cloister between his new buttresses. His instructions were to match his nave to the style of the chancel, but he made no attempt to imitate the remarkable and unique detailing of the magnificent early fourteenth-century work of Abbot Knowles. His nave contains little of the brilliance of his St James the Less, London, or his church at Kingston, but is dull and academic, although the scale is impressive.

Street also refaced and slightly altered the central tower, to its detriment, and inserted a more 'correct' window in place of the seventeenth-century one in the north transept. The west front, the towers of which were completed by Pearson, after Street's death, lacks interest. The detailing is poor and the whole composition has a meagre quality which compares badly with the earlier parts of the building.

*Bristol Cathedral before restoration, with the medieval pulpitum half way down what is now the choir, and (right) looking towards the choir from Street's new nave, with Pearson's screen of 1904*

However, it enabled Bristol to take its rightful place among the out-standing cathedrals of Britain, for which, in its truncated form, it could not qualify. As a nineteenth-century essay in cathedral building it makes an interesting comparison with Pearson's Truro and Bodley's Washing-ton cathedrals, both completed much later, and has considerably more architectural distinction than Sir Arthur Blomfield's reconstruction of the ruinous nave at Southwark.

The efforts of John Loughborough Pearson, one of the greatest Gothic Revival architects, to conserve the cathedrals in his care also left much to be desired. Pearson had a thriving ecclesiastical practice, of which Truro Cathedral, completed by his son, is the outstanding example. The *Builder* of 1874 admired his great church, St Augustine's, Kilburn, which it rightly called 'clever and good'. But in his treatment of cathedrals, he did things which were neither clever nor good. At Rochester he was narrowly prevented by the Society of Antiquaries from replacing the medieval pulpitum by an open stone screen of his own. Scott had removed its charming late eighteenth-century Gothic decoration and Pearson embellished it with niches and statues of inferior quality. The delightful late eighteenth-century organ case was also destroyed at this time.[51] Pearson was responsible for the design of the high altar executed

*Pearson's design for a spire over the crossing tower of Peterborough*

by Farmer and Brindley, some figures of which were rightly said, by Hodgson Fowler, to be 'enough to ruin any design'.[52]

The Norman west front was refaced, refurbished and embellished with new turrets and two new statues. A fifteenth-century octagonal turret was replaced by 'a sham, Norman adaptation by the architect'.[53] Pearson's renewal of the 'Norman enrichments on the outer portion of the west doorway', and of other 'decorative features', caused the Society for the Protection of Ancient Buildings 'regret and amazement', and appears to have been considerably more drastic than the treatment proposed by Scott.[54]

Pearson was called urgently to Peterborough when the central tower showed signs of imminent collapse; cracks had appeared into which it was possible to insert the whole arm. He recommended complete re-building of the central tower and crossing, on the grounds that the central piers were 'of the most wretched construction . . . with scarcely a stone in them larger than a man's hand . . . on no account must any attempt be made to rebuild the tower on these piers'.[55]

Pearson intended to replace the east and west tower arches with 'Norman' ones, like those to the north and south. These 'improvements' were thwarted by the intervention of the SPAB; but nevertheless the tower was soon demolished and a new cornerstone laid in 1884, 'with full masonic pomp', without any idea of the style or form which the new tower would eventually take. The SPAB urged caution: 'For a medieval building is . . . like a house of cards; as soon as you interfere with the construction of one part, it is almost certain to set other parts moving.'[56] The controversy raged in the columns of *The Times*; many of the leading architects of the day were involved. J. P. Seddon urged that: 'Mr Pearson, an architect in whom we all have confidence . . . [should be allowed to] . . . write his page in the history of the cathedral.'[57] T. G. Jackson wrote: 'Neither he [Pearson], nor anyone else in this age is qualified to add a fresh chapter to that stone book, which should now be closed for ever.'[58] Professor Freeman, the historian, said feelingly: 'We do not want a new Minster of Peterborough, even though it were to be a much better one than the present one. We want to keep that Minster of Peterborough which is the result of the actual history of Peterborough.'[59] The dilemma was eventually resolved by the Archbishop of Canterbury, who pronounced that a straightforward rebuilding should be carried out, with provision, if necessary, for the erection of an octagon, or some other superstructure; so the compromise so dear to English hearts was reached, and many of the old stones were used.

Pearson had designed a high tower, topped by a splendid spire; but the Bishop threatened to withdraw his subscription if the work was carried out, and the idea was abandoned, perhaps regrettably, since the existing squat tower is even less imposing than its predecessor. An extra Norman arcaded storey was then agreed to, but never carried out. During the long period between the demolition of the tower and its eventual reconstruction, exposure to the elements caused considerable damage to the great painted ceiling of the nave. Pearson's painted vault to the central tower is, however, very fine.

No sooner had this controversy died down than another sprang up, occasioned by the damage caused to the gables of the west front by a storm. In the end Pearson had his way and the upper section of the west front was entirely rebuilt, against the advice of many distinguished architects. Philip Webb, on behalf of the SPAB strongly advocated the strengthening of the existing gables with concrete and ties, but this advice was rejected, to the fury of the preservationists.

Lord Grimthorpe, although no architect, cannot be omitted from this survey, for his amateurish alterations at St Albans, for which he paid around £100,000, were probably the most destructive ever perpetrated upon a cathedral. The *Builder*[60] called his new south transept front 'railway station gothic', and accused Grimthorpe of being 'an architectural pretender who can pay for the privilege of amusing himself . . . with a building which is the property of the nation'.[61] His new rose window, which replaced a Perpendicular one, was referred to by a contemporary as a 'stone colander'.[62]

Morris, in 1884, made the following sweeping condemnation of the restoration: 'As it goes on a terrible dullness settles on this once romantic and deeply interesting building. The new roof is dull, the west front is more dull, the changes of style in the long south side now fail to raise the slightest emotion, since they are so obviously the work of one time . . . the whole is . . . an architectural freak.'[63]

T. G. Jackson is chiefly famous for his Examination Schools at Oxford, and for his ingenious additions to Brasenose and Trinity Colleges, Oxford. However, his brilliant restoration of Winchester Cathedral (1905–12) marked a new era in architectural first aid. A diver was for the first time used to inspect the foundations. With his help it was discovered that the presbytery and Lady Chapel, then in a very serious state of decay, had been built on horizontal tree trunks, laid on the marsh with no foundations whatever. Concrete sacks were lowered down through the water, placed in position under the walls, and the building successfully underpinned. The vaulting of the Lady Chapel, which had subsided, was lifted with tie rods, thus obviating the rebuilding that many architects might have thought necessary. The south nave aisle was found to be falling outwards: its foundations were concreted and the present flying buttresses erected. The cost was £113,000, a considerable sum for that date.

G. F. Bodley, whose work on cathedrals was largely confined to decoration, believed that art required the 'salt of noble sentiment to keep it elevated and pure'.[64] He condemned the futile attempt to outdo the works of the past by coarseness and 'what is vulgarly called "go" in design' and believed that 'if there is one principle in the practice of architecture in the present day which is chiefly wanting, it is, I think . . . refinement of design'.[65] His figures on the medieval reredos at Winchester certainly exhibit this quality and are greatly preferable to much nineteenth-century ecclesiastical statuary. However he, in his turn, was condemned by Richard Norman Shaw:

Is it possible that this can be great art – I fear not, and yet it is a good work of Bodley's, a man we both sincerely admire . . . [But] can nineteenth-century work . . . consist in a servile copy of the fifteenth century? Real work must, I contend, be living work. . . . There is absolutely no idea in such a thing as that screen. It is simply . . . down to the minutest detail, a clean copy.[66]

With these words Shaw finally rejected the medieval movement and all that it stood for.

Sir Arthur Blomfield, another late Victorian restorer, was chiefly famous for his domestic buildings. He was therefore a surprising choice for the rebuilding of the nave at Southwark; as at Bristol, there was very little of the original fabric left. His solution, though heavy and dull, is in its own way competent, and has saved a major building that might, after many vicissitudes, have been lost altogether.

At Canterbury, the SPAB was in the forefront of a controversy over Blomfield's re-painting of the chapter house, which rendered it 'entirely like . . . a brand new building'.[67] A subscriber to the restoration fund wrote, anonymously, to the Society, complaining that: 'It seems

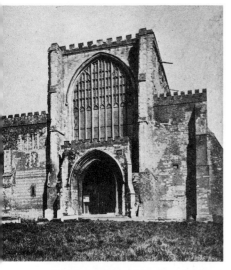

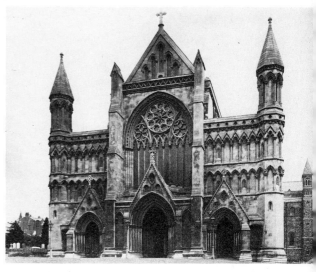

*The west front of St Albans Cathedral before and after restoration by Lord Grimthorpe*

*Lord Grimthorpe's rose window in the N. transept of St Albans, referred to as the 'stone colander'*

hardly possible that an architect [Sir Arthur Blomfield] should have committed such an error in a scheme for artistic decoration which nearly converted the Chapter House into a music hall.'[68]

What conclusions emerge from this survey of the treatment architects of the nineteenth century gave our cathedrals? The significant factor, common to them all, was that they had developed their own theories of Gothic before embarking on cathedral restoration. They were also demonstrating confidence in their ability to improve upon the medieval tradition, a very Victorian thing to do.

The architect has always had the moral choice of adoption or replacement. Cathedrals, incorporating outstanding architecture of many periods, pose this problem in its acutest form. No one should exert moral judgment over the styles of other periods; yet this is precisely what architects over the years have always done; hence the theme of this book. Given the fact that a cathedral has a function for which it must be maintained, what were the options open to them? Owing to the iconoclasm of the seventeenth century and the neglect of the eighteenth, the nineteenth century inherited these problems of evaluation in an extreme form. The conservative repairs recommended by Ruskin and the Society of Antiquaries, and later by Morris and the SPAB, are, we hope, accepted today as the only moral solution, but to architects they have seldom appealed. To the Ecclesiologists such arguments did not exist, and it was their introduction of stylistic and liturgical theories that proved so disastrous to nineteenth-century restoration, and led architects to employ stylistic effects which were often quite out of character with the buildings to which they were attached.

It is sad that both the Cambridge Camden Society and the Oxford Tractarian Movement, created in order to revivify and purify the Church of England, should have become so destructive. Their interest in ritual gave rise to liturgical reforms that led to the destruction of many valuable church furnishings of earlier periods and, by another poignant irony, to a demand for pseudo-medieval artefacts which eventually destroyed the genuine craft tradition.

Beresford Hope, Chairman of the Ecclesiological Society, summed up the dilemma in 1864:

The Art Movement of the last thirty years – the Gothic movement, in one word – of which the pioneers were Pugin and Barry, who have so many noble followers in this room today, created, in Gothic buildings especially, a great and sudden demand for sculpturesque Art inside and outside of the structures. That demand for sculpturesque Art had to be met somehow or other: people had to be found to do it, or the persons who ordered the buildings would have been dissatisfied. Education towards that result was not forthcoming; capital towards it was ready and abundant: and thus has grown up a system of what may be called Art on commission, carried out by middlemen under the direction of the architect. . . . Do not call it Art-practice, but Art-manufacture – then it is all right.[69]

*Southwark Cathedral, before and after restoration by Sir Arthur Blomfield*

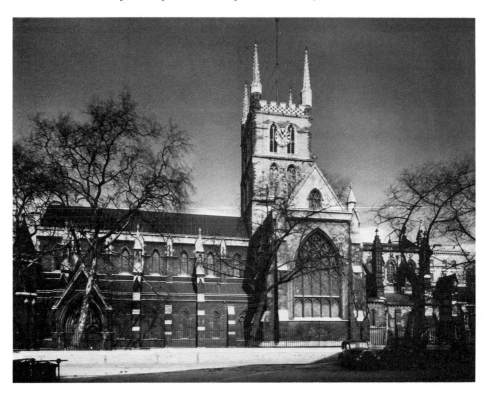

The extent to which it was all right is a matter of opinion; William Morris, who, more than any other man improved the quality of Victorian ecclesiastical design, said of the Art Movement: 'All the minor arts were in a state of complete degradation, specially in England, and accordingly, in 1861 ... I set myself to reforming all that.'[70] His impact on the sterile field of industrial church art will be discussed later. Scott, one of the principal exponents, boasted that 'the subsidiary arts of architectural sculpture, and carving, decorative painting, stained glass, metal work, encaustic tiles . . . are making advances more or less concurrently with architecture itself';[71] a claim that Morris would have denied. Scott's over-confidence destroyed much medieval fabric and nearly eliminated the ecclesiastical craftsmen altogether. The effect of this mechanical art on our cathedrals was particularly destructive. The Gothic Revival must be judged as much by the repetitive and derivative decoration which it produced, as by its architectural theories, for the impact on existing buildings was equally great.

The interest in medieval tiles aroused by Scott's discovery of the great medieval tiled floor at Westminster Abbey, gave encouragement to a flourishing new industry. Scott says, of his discovery: 'The floor of the chapter house is probably the most perfect, and one of the finest encaustic tile pavements now remaining. It is, happily, in a nearly perfect state, having been protected by a wood flooring. . . . Many of the patterns have been pretty correctly copied by Mr Minton in the pavement of the Temple church,'[72] where Sidney Smirke replaced a genuine medieval floor with modern encaustic tiles copied from medieval designs from Westminster. Scott based his reconstruction of the original form of the rose windows at Westminster on sets of four tiles in the chapter house. He also systematically replaced existing floors with new encaustic tiles in most of the cathedrals in which he worked, providing yet another example of the Victorian conviction that a modern copy was as good as, if not better than, the original. Godwin, a manufacturer who worked frequently for Scott between 1848 and 1875, re-tiled the floors of ten English, one Scottish and three Welsh cathedrals. Although he preserved sections of the original marble floor at Ely, Scott replaced a Georgian marble floor at Durham with a new one based on the great Cosmati marble floor in front of the high altar at Westminster, which he had recently restored, thus providing further examples of a tendency to introduce scholarly substitutes, often at the expense of features of genuine antiquity.

Sculpture too suffered from the same fatal lack of spontaneity which had been so accurately diagnosed by Ruskin. 'Frankness is in itself no excuse for imitation; in architecture, nobler and surer signs of vitality must be sought, signs independent of decorative or original character of style. Of these signs, a certain neglect or contempt of refinement in execution, or a visible subordination of execution to conception.'[73] Through his sponsorship of the O'Shea brothers Ruskin attempted to prove that the craft of the medieval sculptor was not dead, and his architectural drawings were a potent factor in drawing attention to genuine Gothic mouldings and statuary. But here again the interest in sculpture thus aroused often led to its wholesale replacement.

At Rochester chapter house doorway, Cottingham gave a headless female statue of 'The Church', the head of a bishop, which Scott later replaced by a female head more suited to the body. Other cathedrals suffered from almost total replacement of statuary of earlier periods. Decayed medieval statues, and decorative carvings, were ruthlessly destroyed and nineteenth-century 'medieval' sculpture took their place. Pfyffers, Boulton, Redfern, Humbolt, Tinworth and Farmer and Brindley were all responsible for an enormous output of statuary, much of it of unprecedented sentimentality, and often of very low artistic quality.

Morris said, of Scott's statuary (by Redfern) on the north portal of Westminster Abbey:

If we hand our monuments down to them (posterity), pretending to be what they are not, we shall both puzzle and discourage them. What will posterity say to the carving of the restored north porch of Westminster Abbey? What credulous empty heads they will think us, who have praised the thirteenth century to them. What they will say is this starved work, these smooth, tame, rubbed-down pieces of stone, that are like nothing that is, or could be in nature, that are neither useful, beautiful, nor suggestive, is this the handiwork of the thirteenth century, of those men of eager hearts and skilful hands, the inheritors of long unbroken ages of skill and love of beauty, is that all they could do?[74]

The medieval practice of representing contemporary characters in stone was revived during the nineteenth century, sometimes with distressing results. Pfyffer's absurd statues of Queen Victoria and Prince Albert on the west front of Canterbury must be one of the most incongruous groups to be found on any of our ecclesiastical buildings. Harry Hems's statues on the altar screen at St Albans, which include at the rear a Virgin with a remarkable resemblance to Queen Victoria, fall into the same category.

At Lichfield, Scott's west front was peopled with repetitive statues, for which the price was adjusted according to the type and position of the character portrayed. This is surely the only example of a Dean and Chapter selling space on the west front of a cathedral, though carried out with the usual idealism. At least they were an improvement on their stucco predecessors.

The appeal stated:

The average cost of the Figures is estimated at not less than £45 each. Those which it is proposed to place in the higher stage of the Tower may probably be obtained for a somewhat less sum. The Dean and Chapter will thankfully accept offers from any who would undertake the amount sufficient for a

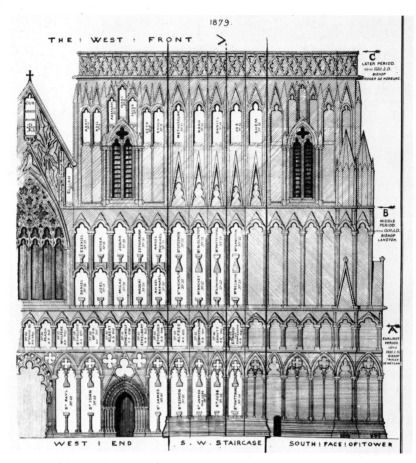

*Diagram of the west front of Lichfield Cathedral showing the position of statues for which private donors were solicited*

Figure from amongst their Friends. The choice of the figures could be left, as far as it can be arranged, to the Donors. But the Dean and Chapter are obliged to reserve to themselves the selection of the sculptors, and the arrangement of all the details of the work, for the sake of securing general uniformity of plan.[75]

Saddest of all, a fine contemporary statue of Charles II, which had replaced a remarkable medieval seated figure of Christ (now in Swinnerton Church), was itself replaced by 'our Lord in Glory' by a local artist, Miss Grant. The Dean and Chapter, in 1884, announced the completion of 'perhaps the most beautiful and elaborate West Front now to be seen in this country'.[76] Scott can be absolved from blame for the statuary, since the responsibility for the sculpture did not come within his contract.

Street, at Bristol, employed Redfern, who produced controversial statues of the four Latin Fathers, including St Gregory wearing a Papal tiara and St Jerome with his cardinal's hat. After a considerable row, the statues were sold to the Tatton-Sykes family, and new ones commissioned. The *Builder* commented: 'It has been an unpleasant affair. . . . For all that, if it should check the use of quiet Romanizing measures now going on all over the country under the guise of artistic decoration, the great body of English people will give hearty thanks.'[77]

Why was most of the statuary produced during the latter half of the nineteenth century of such low artistic quality? The laws of supply and demand, coupled with the architect's requirements for large quantities of unobtrusive statuary, were partly responsible. But the SPAB in 1897, during a controversy over the restoration of Ely Cathedral, perhaps found the answer. 'There does not exist probably in Europe today an artist in stone who could be trusted to repair this defaced sculpture of Alan de Walsingham's craftsmen. For such an artist we must wait for an age, when once more, Art has become not only the expression of a workman's joy in his work, but also the expression of a man of genius who pours into his Art, life, conscience, labour as a sacrificial act of devotion';[78] a statement which certainly derived from the teachings of Morris.

Cathedral glass, much of which was vandalized during the Civil War, also suffered during the late eighteenth and nineteenth centuries. James Wyatt showed his contempt of medieval work by his systematic destruction of thirteenth-century glass at Salisbury. A local glazier at Salisbury complained that 'I expect to beate to peccais a great deal very soon, as it is of now use to me, and we do it for the lead.'[79] Much of it was used to level the close. The rest was thrown into the town ditch. A little of this glass was unearthed during the nineteenth century by a cleric searching the close with a divining rod, and the jumbled pieces were reassembled in one window. At Durham, Wyatt removed the fifteenth-century glass during his reconstruction of the east rose window. Later, such pieces as had not been stolen (for it lay about in baskets for many months) were put back 'with the addition of numerous pieces of modern red, yellow, green, blue, fitted into the window by a jumbling process, looking like a kaleidoscope'.[80]

This vandalism was later matched by Pearson, who mutilated the rare painted glass of 1723, in the north rose window at Westminster, in order to adapt it to his newly designed tracery.

The glass was . . . unique for its date, and . . . the best example of English glass painting in the eighteenth century which we had. . . . A promise was given that the glass should be adapted to the new window, and so it has been, with a vengeance. . . . None of it occupies the place it did before, and the figures of our Lord and the Apostles have positively been cut off short at the feet to make them fit Mr Pearson's new tracery lights.[81]

While architects of the eighteenth century were usually insensitive to the qualities of medieval stained glass, Gothic Revival architects admired medieval glass, but systematically replaced fine eighteenth-century glass by neo-medieval glass, and the destructive cycle was complete. Small wonder that very little historic glass of any period survived.

During his early career Scott commissioned large quantities of glass from Wailes, a former Newcastle grocer; their collaboration at Ely was particularly successful. Street also used Wailes's glass extensively, most notably at Boyn Hill. After 1856 Scott patronized Clayton and Bell, and Hardman, for whom J. H. Powell frequently designed, and from them, Scott obtained some distinguished windows. Occasionally, as at Worcester Cathedral, he planned the overall design for an important window; that of the great west window, which was then implemented by J. H. Powell.

Pugin designed much of his own glass, which was then executed by Willement, Wailes and Hardman; unfortunately much of Hardman's glass in the early 1850s faded badly. (John Hardman and J. H. Powell also designed glass for the firm.)

Burges commissioned glass from Saunders, who designed and made much of the glass for his St Finbarr's Cathedral in Cork. For his east end windows at Waltham Abbey Burges went to the young Burne-Jones; it was executed by Powell, and is the most successful example of their collaboration. Street commissioned glass from Wailes; he also used Henry Holiday, an artist of considerable originality, who designed for Powells, Heaton, Butler and Bayne, and Morris and Co. Clayton and Bell, and Wailes executed a number of Street's own designs. Bodley patronized C. E. Kempe, and Morris and Co. Other notable nineteenth-century glass designers were Westlake (who designed for Lavers and Barraud), Kempe, Willement, and Burlison and Grylls.

At its best, Victorian glass was extremely fine, displaying a range of colour and of subjects not attempted since the fifteenth century. Unfortunately too much inferior glass was manufactured, giving the whole industry a thoroughly bad name. It was Burne-Jones who transformed the manufacture of stained glass. His sense of colour, and the startling originality of his designs (especially during his early career, when he designed for Powells), introduced a new dimension and revitalized an art form which had lost its inspiration. Later when he became the principal designer for Morris and Co., the Italianate influence became more marked.

His glass never became stylized, and his designs for the Four Evangelists at Jesus College, Cambridge, and for St Martin, Brampton, by Philip Webb derive their inspiration unmistakably from the Sistine Chapel and have much more in common with much seventeenth-century glass than with the more predictable Victorian glass.

In the early days of Morris and Co. some of the glass was designed by Morris himself, and by Marshall, Madox Brown, Rossetti, Albert Moore and Simeon Solomon. Their designs and the techniques used,

*Inigo Jones's classical screen for Winchester Cathedral (now in the Archaeological Museum, Cambridge) and Scott's replacement of 1873*

represented a complete breakaway from the Victorian tradition. The subjects chosen, the miraculously subtle gradations of colour and the freshness of approach single out Morris glass unmistakably from the sentimentality and harshness of much Victorian glass.

Later in the century, when pale glass became fashionable, and Clayton and Bell's output changed markedly, Morris glass still retained its subtle and varied range of colours.

The sudden revival of interest in liturgy aroused by the Ecclesiologists created a demand for Gothic church furniture on an unprecedented scale. Some architects, such as Sedding and Street, designed each item individually, and personally supervised its construction. Scott relied for work of quality on craftsmen such as Skidmore, yet lent his name to much that was inferior.

The Ecclesiological movement made itself felt, above all, in the furnishings of chancels. The placing of screens, altars, stalls and organs has been the subject of continual debate and change of fashion, and more destruction has occurred here, in the name of liturgical reform, than anywhere else. Some of the medieval screens, that survived the Reformation and Cromwell's iconoclasts, were destroyed in the eighteenth century in favour of the through vista, or converted to 'Gothick', only to be replaced in the nineteenth century by elaborate wood, metal or stone screens in the full Gothic Revival of Scott, Pearson and the rest. The destructive cycle was complete. Today, as the 'single room', open-plan cathedral returns to favour, screens are again on the

*Choir of Salisbury Cathedral showing (left) Wyatt's fittings and (right) Scott's. Scott's screen was destroyed in 1959*

way out, and the Victorian Society fights to retain the very screens by Scott which Morris fought to keep out. With each change, valuable work is lost. The SPAB summed up the problem in 1891, over a controversy at Tewkesbury:

When our fine cathedrals and abbey churches had screens the clergy did their utmost to get them removed, and now that they are gone, as great an effort is needed to prevent new ones from being erected as to save the old ones from being removed. If people really saw the true worth of our medieval churches they would realize how dangerous it is to introduce new work into old buildings. It is like putting new wine into old bottles, for both are destroyed.[82]

Several mutilated medieval stone altar screens survive: at Winchester, St Albans and Southwark, the niches were renewed, and peopled with statues designed by Bodley, Hems and Blomfield respectively, with varying success. The Perpendicular choir screen at Chichester, removed by Slater during his refurbishing of the chancel, has recently been reinstated, and much of Slater's work removed.

One of the worst disasters was the removal of Inigo Jones's great screen at Winchester in 1819 by Garbett, whose stone pulpitum was, unfortunately, in its turn demolished in 1873, in favour of Scott's ugly black oak screen. At Ely James Essex removed the Norman stone pulpitum, the earliest surviving in England, and replace it by one of his own design, also later destroyed by Scott. At Peterborough the

*Choir of Westminster Abbey showing (left) Wren's high altar, removed by Wyatt, and (right) the crossing and chancel with Scott's fittings*

magnificent 'reredos of carved stone, painted, gilt and inlaid with plates of silver',[83] was destroyed by Cromwell's troops, and replaced after two successive reredoses by Blore's altar screen.

Wyatt, at Lichfield, removed the Gothic stone choir screen (parts of which were incorporated into a new organ screen) and the classical reredos, much admired by Celia Fiennes, in 1697. A freestone altar, 'elegantly sculptured'[84] by Wyatt, was placed against the east end of the Lady Chapel. After complaints from the organist of having to play 'in the severest cold weather when very often there was only one vicar . . . and an old woman at church', a new glazed screen was erected in 1801, in front of the organ, reaching to the roof. This must have improved the plight of the organist,[85] but led to the complaint that 'It is all seeing and no hearing'.[86] Wyatt also filled in the arches of both choir aisles, creating a room within the cathedral – referred to as 'the finest drawing room in Europe'.[87] The nave became redundant, as was fairly usual at this time. Scott later displaced all Wyatt's Gothick fittings, and reversed the arrangements to conform with Ecclesiological requirements.

At Salisbury Wyatt removed the stone pulpitum, which was successively replaced first by his stone screen, and then by a particularly fine decorative metal screen of Scott's, itself removed in 1959, and subsequently destroyed. The Friends of Salisbury justified this on the grounds that 'in consequence the architecture of the Cathedral has been allowed to speak for itself'.[88]

At Hereford Scott replaced a medieval stone screen with an extremely elaborate one of his own design, executed by Skidmore, which was also recently removed, despite protests from the Victorian Society. At Bristol, the 'frightful Corinthian' reredos was thrown out, revealing mutilated medieval work which was repaired and 'elaborately gilt and coloured'.[89] The present reredos was erected to Pearson's design, farther west, in 1899.

At Westminster Abbey, Wyatt removed Wren's splendid high altar, with 'massive corinthian columns', and decoration by Grinling Gibbons, originally in the chapel of Whitehall Palace. The replacement, a 'reconstruction' of the medieval reredos by Wyatt and Bernasconi, carried out in Roman cement, was itself replaced by Scott. (Under Wyatt, there was also a proposal to replace the statue of Aymer de Valance in the sanctuary, with one of General Wolfe. Horace Walpole offered to accommodate Aymer at Strawberry Hill, and also at the request of the Dean put forward ideas for a new openwork altar screen.[90])

At Tewkesbury, Scott removed 'all post-medieval excrescences', including the galleries in the transepts,[91] and gave the interior a thorough overhaul. The altar, 'a slab of blue marble, said to be the most beautiful in England, had been removed, in 1739, at night, sawn in two, and turned into benches on either side of the porch. Scott reinstated it, reframed in oak.'[92] This disgraceful example of the lack of respect shown to churches during the eighteenth century also illustrates the care which Scott frequently took to reinstate original features of value, when they were medieval. He was less scrupulous with later work.

The same sequence can be traced throughout our cathedrals, and merely proves the vulnerability of cathedral furnishings. The Victorian commercialization of religious furnishings frequently led to a meaningless repetition of medieval motifs, applied mechanically, without understanding. The supply of medieval examples was so limited that their reproduction tended to resolve itself into a mere repetition. This was particularly true of church plate. Pugin, Burges and Street created designs of power and originality, but the craft later deteriorated into mere copying. Only with the arrival of Ashbee and Henry Wilson was a new style evolved.

It was as a reaction to the deterioration of church decoration that Morris and Burne-Jones, inspired perhaps by their initial training for the priesthood, created the Arts and Crafts movement. Burne-Jones, who was deeply aware of the ecclesiastical implications of the movement, admits the source of his inspiration when he says: 'If I took account of my life, and the days in it that most went to make me, the Sunday at Beauvais [Cathedral] would be the first day of creation.'[93]

As Burges and Street attempted to translate the medievalism of the Pre-Raphaelites into bricks and mortar, so Morris and Burne-Jones, who were responsible for the survival of the movement, breathed new life into the sterile field of Victorian church art. Burne-Jones's influence

*Hereford Cathedral, the choir screen by Scott and Skidmore, recently dismantled and removed*

on the development of stained glass has already been mentioned. He also re-invigorated the design of tapestry. Morris, however, admitted that, in Morris and Co., 'almost all the designs we use for surface decoration, wallpapers, textiles and the like, I design myself'.[94] He also acknowledged the inspiration that his genius found in natural forms, with the following testimony:

Everything made by man's hands has a form which must be beautiful or ugly . . . beautiful if it is to accord with nature and helps her; ugly if it is discordant with nature, and thwarts her. . . . It is one of the chief uses of decoration . . . that it has to sharpen our dulled senses in this matter; for this end are those wonderful intricate patterns interwoven, those strange forms invented . . . in which the hand of the craftsman is guided to work . . . till the web, the cup, or the knife, look as natural, nay lovely, as the green fields, the river bank, or the mountain flint.[95]

The tradition established by Morris and Co. for naturalism and pride in craftsmanship was continued with equal fervour by Ashbee, Wilson and Gimson. Wilson, in 1899, spoke of 'a whole generation of artists going on their way neglected by the Church . . . the Church . . . has been captured by commercialism,'[96] and Ashbee said:

the history of every country for a thousand years has no fact so important as the change from domestic to factory industry. The disappearance of the small workshop, with the Guild system that regulated human labour and set its standard of quality in life and in the work of man's hands, is more far-reaching than any religious or dynastic change. But the Arts and Crafts movement made the Discovery that it was only in the small hand workshop that those things could be had again for which that movement stood.[97]

William Morris expressed this more forcibly when he said of church furnishings: 'Will not every piece of modern work make "the old place" (the church, I mean) look less old and more like a nineteenth century medieval furniture dealers' warehouse.'[98] Morris was, in his capacity as a craftsman, opposed to the inferior design of much cathedral decoration, for which industrialization was responsible. He was also, as a connoisseur of architecture, contesting the insensitivity of cathedral restoration. It was through his efforts that both the Arts and Crafts movement and the preservation movement were born, as we see in more detail elsewhere in this book. Both were brought into being as a direct result of the 'restoration disease', which raged for over a hundred years. Morris shared with Ruskin a particular concern for the historical importance of old buildings as truthful records of the past; and both were out of sympathy with the work of many Gothic Revival architects. Ruskin's largely abortive attempts to combat cathedral restoration, and to endow a preservation fund through the Society of Antiquaries, are referred to elsewhere in this book. Paradoxically, he was attempting to protect medieval buildings, not from classicists, but from medievalists, who were proving more destructive than the stylistic destroyers of the past.

Morris's Society for the Protection of Ancient Buildings arrived, alas, too late, when the mainspring of the Gothic Revival had run down. However, the church authorities were indignant at the violent reactions provoked by their well-meaning attempts to improve the buildings in their care. The Rev. E. T. Yates, from Aylsham, Norfolk, accused the Society of Antiquaries of throwing 'unjust and unwarranted stigma on many persons who have during the past ten or twelve years, been . . . desirous of promoting the glory of God . . . by affording increases and improved accommodation in our churches'. He pointed out that churches

are not set apart for the collection of antiquities, or merely for the preservation of the records of past ages, but for the worship of Almighty God. Many of our churches . . . had nearly fallen into ruin, and are very ill-adapted through their internal fittings to meet the requirements of the present age; and what is the preservation of a few antiquated relics to the general welfare of the public?[99]

The clash of interests was to occur later when William Morris referred to churches as 'ecclesiastical toys', and the Dean of Canterbury accused him of regarding his cathedral as 'a place of antiquarian research or for budding architects to learn their art in. We need it for the daily worship of God'.[100]

Of course, by no means all the damage done in the nineteenth century was in the name of restoration. The Industrial Revolution often crept perilously near to cathedral precincts. In 1854 the Society of Antiquaries sent a memorial to Lord Palmerston, as Home Secretary, on the importance of preserving monuments in churchyards threatened by railway companies. Norwich Cathedral close was, at this time, being menaced by a project for a new railway development, and a new approach road to Rennie's London Bridge threatened the Lady Chapel at Southwark Cathedral.

In 1860 the Society attacked the Dean and Chapter of Worcester for the proposed demolition of the Guesten Hall (which in fact happened) and in 1870 protested against the proposed removal of the choir screens at Exeter and Wakefield, and, at the same time, supported Scott's restoration of the chapter house at Westminster. The first Commissioner of Works, in 1869, requested the Society to 'furnish a list of such Regal and other Historical Tombs or Monuments existing in Cathedrals, Churches and other Public Places and buildings as in their opinion it would be desirable to place under the protection and supervision of the Government, with a view to their proper custody and protection'.[101]

The Society agreed, and, in 1872, issued a list of the more important monuments in all the counties of England before 1760. When the government refused to take any action, the Society insisted that their report should be laid before Parliament. The agitation that followed resulted in the setting up of the Royal Commission on Historical Monuments; a recording, but not a protective body. This was, however, the first step towards the concept of the Statutory List, on which all our protective legislation is based today. The Society were advised to be cautious in committing themselves to any proposal for withdrawing the custody of ancient monuments from Deans and Chapters of cathedrals, as such a proposition would arouse the keenest opposition.[102] These authorities still retain total control of all cathedral fabrics, a hundred years later, despite consistent efforts to bring them under the protection of the planning laws: a strange and worrying anachronism.

The year 1877 was a landmark in the history of preservation, for Lubbock's Ancient Monuments Bill passed its second reading in Parliament, and Morris founded the Society for the Protection of Ancient Buildings, as a protest against the poposed restoration at Tewkesbury Abbey. One of his first manifestos read: 'That in view of the deplorable falsification that has been for long going into ancient buildings in the name of restoration, this Society deserves the support of all those who are interested in art, archaeology and history.'[103] At the first meeting of the Society this resolution was passed: 'That ancient buildings are among the most valuable records of national history and progress and, as such, are worthy of the utmost care of the public and of individuals, the loss of which is definite and irreparable.'[104] In 1878 the Rev. T. W. Norwood wrote poignantly:

It is melancholy to see old armorial glass taken out of the windows of a chantry and put into a conservatory, to see decorated tracery wantonly broken, inadequate and unworthy attempts at reproduction; or distressing combinations of old forms, separated from their environments, and so despoiled of their grace and significance. Much posterity will find to praise in the reign of Queen Victoria; much will they praise our science, our inventions, the improvements of our civilisation, in every kind; but this one thing they will for ever deplore, the irretrievable loss of that which above all things they would have desired to see, the unbroken link of our ancient art.[105]

In December 1887 the SPAB decided to send 'to the Archibishops, Bishops and Chancellors of Dioceses, Deans and Archdeacons and Rural Deans of the Church of England' a letter drawing their attention to the destruction of ancient monuments under the name of restoration.
It said:

It is constantly the case that on visiting a 'restored' Church it is found that monuments and painted glass, of which the existence is recorded in County Histories, have not only been removed from their original positions, but are no longer forthcoming; that inscribed slabs from tombs have been used to bridge over the gutters or to receive hot-air gratings, or have been covered with tiles; that the ancient fonts have been removed, the old communion tables destroyed, and the Jacobean oak pulpits broken up or mounted on stone pedestals, and not infrequently the old and curious communion plate sold. The architectural features and proportions of the churches have in innumerable instances been modified, especially so far as regards the east windows, and the character of the chancels generally.[106]

A list of unrestored churches was also compiled by the Society at this period; Morris said 'Go round our great cathedrals restored by distinguished architects and see what flaying will do for works of art.'[107]

The words of Morris thundered through the records of the time; the invective was tremendous, but the destruction went on. But by the end of the nineteenth century the tide of restoration had almost run its course. The curtain seemed to have fallen on the 'restoration tragedy'. But we are now witnessing a curious epilogue. The Victorian Society, which is proud of its descent from William Morris, has been largely responsible for the reinstatement of Victorian architecture in public esteem. The contribution made by architects of this period is now accepted, and few would deny that Scott, Street, Burges and Pearson created a corpus of buildings which are valid as works of art, and can stand comparison with the best of any other period. The time may come when their alterations to our cathedrals, mellowed with age, will themselves be admired, and when those buildings so ruthlessly corrected to Middle Pointed will be appreciated for their coherence. Already the Society finds itself fighting to preserve the very decorations and furnishings that Morris deplored, and against which he protested so passionately. And so the battle goes on.

# MARK GIROUARD

*Antony, Cornwall. The Victorian wing (since demolished) is on the left, behind the cedar tree*

# VI  Living with the past: Victorian alterations to country houses

THROUGHOUT the Victorian period, new technologies, new standards of behaviour, new social conventions and fashions and a great deal of new money came pouring into the spacious country house world. Existing country houses were, as a result, under enormous pressure. One has to remember this when considering what the Victorians did to the country houses, historic or otherwise, which they inherited. If not the last period when the country house way of life was flourishing, theirs was certainly the last period when its spatial demands were increasing. It was not only that the planning and technical equipment of older country houses failed to measure up to new standards; they were, in many cases, painfully too small. And so it came about that Victorian landowners, when not rebuilding their houses, were busily engaged in altering, enlarging or modernizing them. Architecturally the results were sometimes distressing, but by no means always so. There is, I think, a widespread belief that the Victorians did terrible things to country houses; the theme of this article is that they were more often cautious and conservative than arrogantly destructive.

But the evidence for those Victorian alterations which came short of a complete remodelling is not easy to assemble. It is the completely Victorian or Victorianized houses which attracted the attention of building journals in their own day, and architectural historians of the present. Houses which were mangled by the Victorians are, by and large, ignored; the best place to find them is in the advertisement pages of *Country Life*, where they are described as 'suitable for school or other institutional use'. Even in the houses which make the editorial pages, any Victorian embellishments tend to be tastefully cut; the camera is carefully angled so as to leave them out; the plans do not show the Victorian service wings, and additions to the main house are shown only in outline; by the time many houses are featured, Victorian additions have already been removed. Occasional articles (e.g. on Buscot Park, Berkshire, in 1940)[1] actually celebrate the de-Victorianization of a house, with before and after photographs; these are of considerable interest to a Victorian historian, but even here the pre-alteration plans and photographs tend not to be nearly as detailed as one might wish. The splendidly detailed plans published in the Royal Commission on Historical Monuments volumes, with different hatchings for work of different dates, usually show Victorian work in outline or under the relatively useless heading of 'after 1800'; this may make sense according to their terms of reference, but considerably reduces their value as social documents. (And it is from the social rather than the aesthetic point of view that these Victorian alterations and additions are fascinating to study.) As a result I am all too well aware that the remarks that follow rest on a basis of evidence much less comprehensive than I would have wished.

### Alterations of convenience

The reasons that led a Victorian landowner to enlarge, alter or rebuild his house were numerous, but can be divided into two main classes, of taste and of convenience. The two classes overlap. Most Victorian owners who remodelled or rebuilt their houses primarily for aesthetic reasons took the opportunity to rearrange or add to their accommodation; and additions made in the first place for convenience sometimes ended in a complete visual remodelling. Nevertheless, the distinction can be made, and as convenience was, I believe, rather more important than aesthetics, I am dealing with it first.

There were increasing numbers of features which Victorian owners were unable to accept in their servants' quarters, whether for reasons of propriety, their own comfort, the comfort of their servants or just a sense of orderliness. They disliked kitchens in the basement under their own part of the house, because it made them vulnerable to kitchen smells; they disliked men servants sleeping close to women servants, or any servants sleeping in dormitories together; they disliked laundry maids working close to the grooms. They wanted their boots blacked, their silver polished, their newspapers ironed and their lamps trimmed; standards were higher than they had been in the eighteenth century and for all these activities they required a separate space, and often a separate room. They had to put up increasing numbers of visiting servants (for virtually everyone who came to stay brought a personal servant) in increasing comfort. They required more in the way of larders and sculleries for their kitchens, and more extensive laundries. What it all added up to was that the existing servants' quarters in pre-Victorian houses had to be at the least reorganized, often enlarged and frequently rebuilt on a much more lavish scale.

The gentry-end of the house was also under pressure in Victorian times. It was a pressure often made evident in the act of arrival, when a new *porte-cochère* shielded visitors from the weather and an additional front hall or vestibule, with toilets alongside it, kept draughts out of the house and provided new facilities for guests. Another almost completely new arrival on the Victorian scene was what I have called elsewhere the male preserve,[2] a quarantine area of the house designed to protect the susceptible ears and noses of Victorian ladies from male smut and male tobacco smoke. The male preserve could vary in size, according to the taste and purse of the owner, from a single billiard-cum-smoking room to an elaborate range consisting of billiard, smoking and gun room, the owner's 'den' and spacious lavatories and washrooms. Thus equipped, a country house was adapted to deal with the male half of the massive Victorian weekend and holiday house-parties which the spread of the railways made increasingly feasible. Such house-parties also required a considerable increase in bedroom accommodation. The large size of many Victorian families provided another reason for more bedrooms, with nurseries and schoolrooms to match. A frequent addition, pre-Victorian in origin but especially rampant in Victorian days, was a conservatory; less frequent was a chapel, only found in ultra-religious households, for according to rigorous tradition the landowner attended Sunday services in his parish church.

Finally, Victorian country houses reflected to a greater or lesser extent improvements in technology. What was done depended very much on the inclination and purse of the owners. But almost all country houses were fitted with new plumbing and drainage in the course of the Victorian period, and many were supplied with gaslight and central heating, at least in the passages or on the ground floor. Electricity began to spread, very slowly at first, in the 1880s and 90s. A frequent 'improvement' and one that visually left its mark as much as any Victorian innovation was the replacement of the original glazing by big sheets of plate glass, and the fitting of external blinds to the windows.

So the natural play of forces tended to leave a Victorianized house with a new, greatly enlarged service wing to one side, and a smaller, but rather more pretentious billiard-room wing to the other; a new entrance hall slapped on the front and a conservatory at the back; an extra storey on top for more bedrooms; a new clock-tower with a water tank under the clock; new plate glass windows in the living rooms; and a complicated and at times unsightly new circulation system of pipes, bringing gas and central heating to the ground floor, bell pulls to all the rooms and hot and cold water to the two bathrooms and housemaid's closet on the upper floors. Against this natural play of forces had to be set the value placed by the owner on the house he was proposing to alter. There were four main approaches in Victorian times, and it depended on this value which approach was adopted and to what extent. The four can be classified as matching in, livening up, shouting down and remodelling.

The meaning of remodelling is clear enough, and is really more conveniently lumped in with the aesthetics-inspired alteration which will be dealt with later. By 'shouting down' is meant making additions in a different style to what was there already, and totally out of sympathy with it. I think many people would think of this as a typically Victorian approach, and yet when one looks for examples they are comparatively

*Trentham, Staffordshire. The eighteenth-century house is surrounded by Barry's additions*

hard to find. Sometimes what appears to be an example turns out to be the first stage of an envisaged total remodelling that was never completed; Nesfield's Gothic wing (of which more later) at Combe Abbey is a case in point. But of course there are examples, and I will give two of them, equally awful. The first is the Jacobethan wing (I don't know the architect) which clumsily disrupts the harmonious symmetry of Antony in Cornwall, and which the *Country Life* photographer understandably tried to hide behind a cedar tree.[3] The second is the appalling mansard roof with its range of overbearing Gothic dormers which E. W. Pugin clamped on top on the chaste Palladian façade of Garendon Park in Leicestershire. The range of rooms in the roof were made necessary because the two floors of the eighteenth-century block beneath it had been thrown into one enormous room; the detailing of this room, and the addition of the roof are only too typical of the younger Pugin's insensitivity.

'Livening up', however, was a more common approach. The technique might also be called, from the name of its most successful practitioners, 'doing a Barry'. It needed, as its starting-off point, the kind of eighteenth-century building which the Victorians described as 'a dull square white house'. The necessary additions could be deployed so as to turn it from a square block into an example of picturesque diversity; a tower was almost an essential, to liven up the skyline. The additions would be made in the classical style, to be in keeping with the original

*Drumlanrig Castle, Dumfriesshire, Scotland, showing the service wings added about 1850*

house, the façades of which would be left largely unaltered. Charles Barry set the fashion at Trentham, in 1834, where he enlarged an early eighteenth-century house by the addition of a new service wing, new entrance halls and approaches and a new range of family apartments. 'The architectural result of these changes,' it was said, 'has been the conversion of a very uninteresting building into a much more worthy successor of old Sir Richard Leveson's Jacobean mansion'.[4] Barry repeated the formula much more simply at Shrublands about 1850, and it was used by his son, E. M. Barry, at Pyrgo Park in 1862 and at Thorpe Abbots in 1869. There are numerous other examples, one of the last of which is H. J. Stevens of Derby's additions to Locko Park, Derbyshire, in the 1850s and 60s.

I can't pretend to have assembled enough statistical evidence but I suspect that the commonest form of Victorian addition was what I have described as 'matching in'. This meant following the style of what was there already, with no attempt to alter or add to the aesthetic content; in many cases it meant exactly repeating the existing detail. The method was followed for houses of all styles, whether Tudor, Elizabethan or classical. Its success depended very much on how tactfully it was done. The two service wings added to Drumlanrig about 1850, for instance, could scarcely have been improved on for self-effacing correctness; they are carefully kept much lower than the main block, accentuate its symmetry, and enclose its forecourt; they are built of the same stone and

*Ammerdown, Somerset, the main block extended in 1857, and the smoking room*

*Petworth, Sussex, the south front remodelled by Salvin, who also added the arched entrance on the right*

with similar detail.[5] Another sensitive example of this kind of addition is at Ammerdown in Somerset.[6] James Wyatt's original house of 1788 was added to twice, in 1857 and 1877. The first addition almost doubled the size of the original main block, but did so with the utmost care by extending the Wyatt elevations and copying his detail so carefully that it is now impossible to see the junction. In 1877 a long wing was added to the north containing a smoking room and servants' rooms. In 1901 a new entrance was made between the smoking room and the main block; the old entrance had been on the west front which was now freed for an extension of the garden. The 1877 wing is long, low and unassuming, with a little tower at the far end and agreeable classical detailing; inside, the smoking room is handsomely classical, with a screen of columns.

The many additions made to older houses by Anthony Salvin in the first half of the period are almost unfailingly tactful. His additions to Encombe, Petworth and Longford Castle, for instance, all made in the years around 1870, strike a praiseworthy balance between conservatism and convenience.[7] At Encombe in Dorset the main entrance was moved from the south to the north, and the new entrance given importance by the addition of a grand central chimney stack, designed in the Vanbrughian manner of the house, and pedimented dormers based on the similar central feature on the south front. On this side of the house no alterations were made, except for the glazing in of the originally open colonnades. Inside, a number of smaller rooms were knocked together to make big reception rooms decorated in an eighteenth-century manner; the staircase was enlarged with balusters of early eighteenth-century type. A long service range, invisible from the south, was inconspicuously added along the west side of the house.

At Petworth, Salvin was engaged to provide three favourite Victorian amenities: family apartments, an improved service wing and a new entrance. He achieved them with the minimum of fuss. The south end of the house was rearranged to provide family apartments, and given a new façade which faithfully reproduces the seventeenth-century detailing of the famous west front. All servant accommodation was fitted into a separate outbuilding parallel to the main block; a link was built between the two, in the form of a triumphal arch which served as a *porte-cochère* to the new main entrance, with passage links to the service wing above and below the archway.

At Longford, Salvin was faced with an Elizabethan house to which considerable damage had been done in the 1820s. A scheme had then been set under way to transform the famous triangular plan into a hexagon, but had got no further than the building of two wings with towers at the angles, in scale and materials completely out of sympathy with the Elizabethan work. Wherever their obtrusive white brickwork could be seen in conjunction with the original house, Salvin refaced them with a copy of the Elizabethan chequerboard of flint and stone. He joined the new tower into the Elizabethan with a low wing containing a new dining room, and added two new gabled bays. All his new work was blended in very skilfully with the Elizabethan. Inside, by roofing over the central court he greatly improved the circulation of the house. The roofed-in court now became the main hall; the big eighteenth-century hall in the middle of the entrance front became redundant, and Salvin replaced it by a much smaller hall and billiard room. The latter filled up the space originally occupied by the asymmetrically placed Elizabethan great hall, which the Georgian hall had replaced. Salvin provided big new reception rooms in the 1820s wing, but in the original house left untouched both the few surviving Elizabethan rooms and the splendid ranges of reception rooms and bedrooms redecorated in the eighteenth century.

There are numerous other houses to which the Victorians added wings inconspicuously and with tact, in a style similar to the old work. Lord Palmerston's additions to Broadlands, including a library decorated in the eighteenth-century style, are a case in point.[8] Another is Smith of Shrewsbury's new wing of 1856 at Buntingsdale in Shropshire, which follows the detailing of the Smith of Warwick house of 1721 as closely as the 1857 wing at Ammerdown follows the Wyatt work.[9] A third is the wing added to Callally Castle in Northumberland around 1890.[10]

*Longford Castle, Wiltshire. Salvin's new wing is on the right and contains the dining room (below)*

*Somerley, Hampshire, showing the single-storey addition along the front*

A rather different case is that of Somerley in Hampshire.[11] This was a relatively modest classical house of 1792–95, to which a colonnade was added in 1818, and a picture gallery in 1850. In 1868–70 the house was much extended by William Burn, for the Earl of Normanton. An extra floor was added to get more bedrooms, and a single storey added along the front, to contain a new smoking room and billiard room. This kind of one-storey addition was popular with the Victorians, and had the advantage that it enabled the billiard room to be given a top light. A similar addition to the garden side contained new drawing rooms. The inspiration for the detailing of all these additions was the original Georgian house; even the 1850 picture gallery was refaced to bring it in harmony with the 1818 colonnade. The final effect was, of course, very different from the starting-off point, but it produced a handsome house.

But there were many cases where Victorian additions, although based in style on what they were added to, notably failed to produce a handsome house. At Bulwell Hall in Nottingham, for instance, the original mid-eighteenth-century house can clearly be seen in the middle of the extensive Victorian additions which imitate its quoins, its window surrounds, the urns on its parapet and its symmetry.[12] The result is depressing, because it is so insensitively done; the enormous size of the additions completely swamps the centre, without adding anything of their own, and all the new and many of the old windows have been filled with plate glass. At Everingham in Yorkshire the addition made to a Carr of York house by the Yorkshire architect James Firth in 1845–48, including a new north wing with a two-storey bay-window and a new

*Everingham, Yorkshire, an eighteenth-century house with additions of 1845–48*

bay-window in the centre of the west front, closely followed Carr's work in their brickwork, the shape of their roofs, and the rusticated surrounds, to the windows; but the result was unfortunate (it has recently been removed) because it disrupted the symmetry of Carr's design and turned a shapely house into a shapeless one.[13]

On the whole Victorian additions tended to disregard symmetry, as at Everingham, rather than extend it, as at Bulwell. A typical example was Whitfield in Herefordshire, where the moderate mid-eighteenth-century house of the Clive family was more than tripled in size in 1852 and 1878–82.[14] The first addition approximately followed the Georgian detail of the centre, though with a dash of Italianate round the corner. A second wing was added in 1878 to the designs of William Chesake of Hereford, and the whole house raised by a storey. The second wing roughly balanced the first one but its fenestration was Elizabethan (perhaps on the excuse of the existence of a modest earlier wing at the back of the Georgian house). But a classical balustrade extending right across the building gave some kind of unity to the large and far from shapely house that finally resulted.

Examples of this kind of Victorian elephantiasis are legion, and on the whole, they make an ugly collection, especially when the additions have been made piecemeal over a number of decades. They are usually ugly, however, not because they are aggressively out of sympathy with what they are added to but because they are insensitively conservative; they are killing the house through caution.

### Alterations of taste

Alterations made by the Victorians for reasons of taste fall into two main classes, restorations and improvements: improvements involving the alteration or remodelling of houses which, from a Victorian point of view, had been wrong from the start and restorations putting a house back to its original rightness.

Not surprisingly, the houses which the Victorians looked on with the least delight were those designed in the previous decades, in the late eighteenth or early nineteenth centuries. Worst of all was Georgian Gothic, which the whole weight of Victorian Gothic Revivalism conditioned people to dismiss as ignorant if not actively vicious. But the simple austerity and restrained good proportions of many Georgian classical houses seemed to them bleak and unwelcoming; and the delicacy of Adam plasterwork appeared effeminate to the muscular tastes of the mid-century, though there was a revived fashion for it in the 1880s. 'The Adelphi Adams,' Lewis Vulliamy wrote to his client R. S. Holford of Westonbirt in 1866 'introduced an attenuated Greek sort of Ornamentation, which has long been considered the worst style – indeed it is never used now.'[15]

In Murray's handbook to Shropshire, Cheshire and Lancashire of 1870, Eaton Hall is described as 'one of the most magnificent seats in Britain; but the style, Florid Ecclesiastical Gothic, was a mistake. It was adopted before Gothic was well understood, and although nearly a million has been expended on it, the result is not satisfactory.' In the ensuing years a second million went on enabling Alfred Waterhouse to make it more satisfactory. Few Victorian landlords would have had any qualms in remodelling a Georgian Gothic design, and Waterhouse's work at Eaton Hall was paralleled by George Gilbert Scott's rather less thorough remodelling of James Wyatt's Lee Priory in 1861. Georgian classical houses, especially the plainer and later ones, received a variety of treatments. Some, like Highclere under Barry, described by his son as an example of the 'comparative flatness and insipidity of bare classicism,'[16] were transformed into a building of totally different appearance and style. Others, like Prestwold, under Burn, were transformed from 'flatness and insipidity' to the more richly modelled classicism that appealed to the Victorians by the addition of moulded surrounds to the windows, parapets and other trimmings.[17] In both these cases the clients ended up with rather more distinguished buildings than they had started with. But less capable architects often merely followed the lines of the existing design, as in the clumsy window surrounds and other adornments added about 1870 to Adam's extension at Great Saxham Hall in Suffolk.

Hanging in the gentlemen's lavatory at Linley Hall, Shropshire, are two spirited drawings now nicely captioned 'A warning to the improver.' They show a scheme got out about 1850 for remodelling the classical house designed by Henry Joynes in 1742. An extra floor rich with

*Linley Hall, Shropshire, and (below) a design for enlargement in the 1850s*

*Drumlanrig Castle, with (below) Sir Charles Barry's scheme for enlargement*

dormers and ornamental ironwork, a cupola, a porch, a *porte-cochère* and an arched and pillared screen concealing the stable block largely obscure the reticent and sophisticated lines of the original façades. This alarming but fortunately unexecuted metamorphosis can be paralleled by Sir Charles Barry's scheme for turning Drumlanrig Castle into a Second Empire château with gardens to match.[18]

But perhaps the most interesting aspect of these two schemes is that they were never executed. It is remarkable, considering the prosperity of the period, how many country houses passed through the Victorian period with no alterations or minor and scarcely noticeable ones. Various reasons can be suggested for this. In the first place, although it is tempting for anyone writing about Victorian architecture to see the period through the eyes of Pugin, Gilbert Scott and the Gothic Revivalists, the country house world was much less exclusive in its tastes. To Scott's strictures on 'cold and proud Palladianism'[19] and Pugin's contempt for the 'Italian house in England',[20] for instance, it is worth contrasting the comment of Augustus Hare, a typical country house habitué of the more cultured variety, on Wentworth Woodhouse in 1872: 'A very stately effect as you approach it, with a truly majestic portico.'[21] In fact Salvin, William Burn and George Devey, the three most successful and select of Victorian country house architects, were all capable of designing in convincing mid-eighteenth-century manner on request.[22]

In the second place there was a very sharp pull of inertia and conservatism in the Victorian landowning classes. Compared to their eighteenth-century equivalents they were far less interested in architecture, and knew much less about it; country houses had enormous prestige in Victorian times but the prestige was social rather than architectural; the trappings of social position, of deferential villagers, model farms and cottages, lodge gates and smoothly gravelled drives, elaborately maintained gardens and quietly efficient servants were to most people of more concern than the minutiae of architectural detail.

Finally, the Victorians had a healthy respect for what one might call architectural purity. Anything that was a complete example of its style had a good chance of survival, even if its style was out of favour at the time. In the country house sphere the Victorians destroyed much that was agreeable, but remarkably little that was important. The great Elizabethan and Jacobean mansions were, of course, largely preserved, but so were the later seventeenth-century ones, and every single surviving work by Vanbrugh. The Victorians destroyed no important Palladian house, and when they did add to them added with the greatest tact. The entrance vestibule added to Holkham is admirably self-effacing, and the service extensions are neatly concealed between the wings. E. B. Lamb's work at Kent's Wakefield Lodge is to all intents and purposes invisible, T. H. Wyatt's additions to Lathom House appear alarming on plan, but in fact they were only one storey high, entirely concealed

*Ford Castle, Northumberland, as Gothicized in the mid-eighteenth century*

behind the colonnades on the entrance front, and very inconspicuous on the garden front. At Castletown, in Ireland, the necessary male domain was obtained by converting the stable lofts in one of the wings; inside, chunky Gothic fireplaces of Irish marble, timbered ceilings and antlered trophies are nostalgically redolent of Victorian masculinity; but outside, Palladian reticence remains unaltered.

Even the work of the late eighteenth and early nineteenth centuries, although totally out of fashion during most of the Victorian period suffered relatively few important casualties. The great majority of Wyatt's and Adam's country house work was left untouched. Even Soane, whose work was incomprehensible to the Victorians, suffered relatively little. Georgian Gothic was more vulnerable, but against the loss of Eaton Hall and the mutilation of Lee Priory can be set the careful preservation of Strawberry Hill and Arbury; and George Eliot's enthusiastic description of Arbury in *Scenes of Clerical Life* is a useful reminder that not all Victorians were patronizing or scornful about work of this period.[23]

Respect for architectural purity, however, could work two ways. Country houses, like churches, received their worst blows from the Victorians in the name of 'restoration'. Restoration meant removing accretions and going back to what was there before, or something that was believed to approximate to it. In church terms it meant, on occasions, pulling down fifteenth-century arcades and rebuilding in 'Early Pointed' on the strength of some surviving lancet windows; and most often of all the stripping out of all eighteenth-century fittings. In country house terms it meant taking out Georgian sash windows from Elizabethan houses and replacing them with stone mullions and transoms, or re-medievalizing inhabited castles which had been domesticated in the seventeenth and eighteenth centuries or given Gothic frills in mid and late Georgian times.

*Ford Castle, Northumberland, after restoration by David Bryce*

The restoration of Elizabethan houses was in train from the very beginning of the Victorian period. It was about 1835 that sash windows appear to have been replaced by mullions and transoms at Mapledurham in Oxfordshire.[24] It may be that a coat of Georgian stucco was removed at the same time and the brickwork was found to have been damaged by the keying-in of the stucco; at any rate the present brick surfaces with their prominent diaper certainly date from the same period. A few years later, in 1838–39, H. P. Powys at the neighbouring Hardwick House similarly replaced the mullions and 'had the walls scraped of the whitening, which the bad taste of a preceding generation had placed over the grand old red brick'.[25]

Thereafter there was probably not a year that passed in which the owner of some Elizabethan or Jacobean house wasn't busy refenestrating or making other alterations in the name of restoration. Restoration was often accompanied by enlargement; for instance, at Charlecote in Warwickshire, the work of over twenty enthusiastic years under Willement and Gibson ended in a house approximately doubled in size.[26] At Charlecote the work was conducted with considerable panache, but all too often a Victorian restoration, in houses as well as churches, scraped off the accumulated texture of several centuries and replaced it with detailing whose mechanically worked stonework and slight differences in proportion remorselessly marked it down as Victorian and brought no compensating gains. A typical example is Chilham Castle in Kent, with its curious crab-shaped Jacobean plan, on which David Brandon laid his heavy hand in 1863. By adding a smoking room, corridors round the entrance court and a new office wing, he made the house a great deal more adapted to Victorian ways of life, but his stylistic alterations, which included taking out Georgian sashes and replacing Elizabethan bow and oriel windows which had been removed about 1820, were done with the minimum of feeling.[27]

In 1842 the beautiful and artistic Louisa Stuart married the Marquess of Waterford and moved to Curraghmore, his home in Ireland. This was externally an eighteenth-century classical house of the plainest variety, described by her mother as 'decidedly ugly, but it is a good thing to be so totally void of a bad sort of taste'.[28] This negative virtue preserved it from any alterations over the next seventeen years (though a subsequent generation added a balustraded parapet, window surrounds and other trimmings in the 1870s). But in 1859 Lord Waterford was killed, leaving Ford Castle in Northumberland to his widow for her life. This former Border stronghold was by Victorian standards only too redolent of 'a bad sort of taste' for it had been much and gaily Gothicized in the mid-eighteenth century. The sequel was almost inevitable. In 1865 Augustus Hare, on one of his indefatigable country house rounds, came to Ford and wrote: 'The gingerbread castle of Udolpho has marched back three centuries, and is now a grand massive building in the Audley End style, but with older towers.' The Scottish architect David Bryce had been called in, and every trace of Strawberry Hill Gothic removed.[29]

There were few inhabited castles which did not undergo a similar treatment during Victorian times, in the course of which the domestications of the early Georgians or the Gothic fantasies of the later were removed. What replaced them was usually just as much of a fantasy, in that it bore little relation to the original state of the castle; but it was, at any rate, scholarly, solid, serious and usually sober (though sobriety was not a quality of the work with which Burges replaced Capability Brown's domestic Gothic façades at Cardiff Castle). At Alnwick Castle, a few miles from Ford, Robert Adam's lacy Gothic entirely disappeared before a formidably feudal assault from Salvin. Salvin became the acknowledged expert at 'restoring' castles, and his hand is much in evidence at Muncaster, Dunster, Warwick and Rockingham. Later examples are Bodley's sober refenestration of Powis Castle *c.* 1885, and the work of the northern architect, L. J. Ferguson of Carlisle, at Naworth *c.* 1880, and Bamburgh in 1894–1905.

### From restoration to preservation

The Naworth commission had been offered to Philip Webb, who gave it up because his clients wanted him to make more alterations to the existing structure than he thought right.[30] Webb was at this time one of the most active members of the Society for the Protection of Ancient Buildings, which had been founded in 1877. The Society radically altered the way people looked at buildings. It made them cease to think of them in the abstract as pieces of design, and look at them as living pieces of history, on which each succeeding generation had left its mark. Once this point of view was adopted, any attempt to 'restore' back to an earlier period was just a piece of forgery, which in addition unforgivably erased the historical value of the building.

*Pitchford, Shropshire, a sixteenth-century house restored to its original appearance by George Devey*

The SPAB point of view, which had been set off in reaction to the excessive restoration of churches, gradually percolated into the country house world, though with effects which were not always what the SPAB would have approved of. The Society was the product of a generation which was increasingly responsive to the texture as well as the forms of old buildings; and it was the texture of mid-Victorian restoration work which most crudely distinguished it from genuine old work. But the result of such sensitivity to texture often meant, in country house terms, not that architects stopped forging but that they forged much more skilfully. The mid-Victorian attitude to historicism was more symbolic than visual; they installed, for instance, mullioned and transomed windows and ribbed plaster ceilings as sign-posts to proclaim 'Elizabethan'; but once the message had been established it did not bother them if the detailed treatment conformed to the taste of their own day. So the plasterwork was much chunkier than anything the Elizabethans would have produced, and the windows had one transom instead of two or three and plate glass instead of leaded lights.

In the second half of the Victorian period 'restoration', if still drastic, was usually much more sensitive. The pioneer in this field was George Devey, who as early as the 1850s was replacing eighteenth-century sashes and making other alterations at Penshurst in such a way that today it is often difficult to decide what is Devey and what is sixteenth-century.[31] In the next three decades Devey, in addition to his enormous output of new country houses, was much in demand to add to or 'restore' old ones. His work in this field varies a good deal, but at its best it is very skilful. The entrance front at Pitchford in Shropshire, for instance, impressively sixteenth-century though it may look, is to a considerable extent a Devey restoration, for the original fenestration had been largely altered in the early nineteenth century.[32] This kind of skill was to be developed even further by the architect-decorator, C. E. Kempe, whose own house, Lindfield Manor, was an amazing example of out-Elizabethanizing the Elizabethans.[33]

In the long run, however, the SPAB frame of mind helped to make more radical changes in the way people looked at country houses. They were increasingly admired as expressions of growth, and the itch to 'restore' away the alterations of intermediate generations grew less strong. The owner of a house that was a rag-bag work of different ages found that, instead of being urged by people of taste to do something about it, he was being congratulated on owning a splendid example of rambling old English charm.

A house of this type is gloriously caricatured by Charles Kingsley in his description of Harthover Place in Chapter I of *The Water Babies*.

For Harthover had been built at ninety different times, and in nineteen different styles, and looked as if somebody had built a whole street of houses of every imaginable shape, and then stirred them together with a spoon.

For the attics were Anglo-Saxon
The third floor Norman
The second Cinque-cento
The first floor Elizabethan
The right wing Pure Doric
The centre Early English with a huge portico copied from the Parthenon.
The left wing pure Boeotian, which the country folk admired most of all,
    because it was just like the new barracks in the town, only three times as big.
The grand staircase was copied from the Catacombs at Rome.
The back staircase from the Taj Mahal at Agra. This was built by Sir John's
    great-great-great-uncle, who won, in Lord Clive's Indian Wars, plenty
    of money, plenty of wounds and not more taste than his betters.
The cellars were copied from the caves of Elephants.
The offices from the Pavilion at Brighton.

And the rest from nothing in heaven, or earth, or under the earth.

So that Harthover House was a great puzzle to antiquarians, and a thorough Naboth's vineyard to critics, and architects, and all persons who like meddling with other men's business, and spending other men's money. So they were all setting upon poor Sir John year after year, and trying to talk him into spending a hundred thousand pounds or so, in building, to please them and not himself. But he always put them off, like a canny North-countryman as he was. One wanted him to build a Gothic house, but he said he was no Goth; and another to build an Elizabethan, but he said he lived under good Queen Victoria, and not good Queen Bess; and another was bold enough to tell him that his house was ugly, but he said he lived inside it, and not outside, and another, that there was no unity in it, but he said that that was just why he liked the old place. For he liked to see how each Sir John, and Sir Hugh, and Sir Ralph, and Sir Randal, had left his mark upon the place, each after his own taste; and he had no more notion of disturbing his ancestors' work than of disturbing their graves. For now the house looked like a real live house, that had a history,

*Hutton-in-the-Forest, Cumbria, a house which escaped the complete remodelling suggested by the architect in 1830*

and had grown and grown as the world grew; and that it was only an upstart fellow who did not know who his own grandfather was, who would change it for some spick and span new Gothic or Elizabethan thing, which looked as if it had been all spawned in a night, as mushrooms are . . .

This was written in 1863 before SPAB days, and it is interesting to see the purist meddling of the architect set against the eclectic conservatism of the owner. Kingsley may have been in advance of his time in expressing this kind of view, but one suspects that one reason so many houses escaped more than minor alterations even in early and mid-Victorian days was this passive opposition of conservatism to fashionable purism. It would be interesting, for instance, to know more of the family background which preserved the medley of medieval, Elizabethan and late seventeenth-century work on the façade of Hutton Castle from Webster of Kendal's attempt to give it a bit of 'unity' in 1830. In the end Salvin was brought in instead of Webster but let very much less loose than in other Border mansions.[34]

Even so Salvin's embellishment went a good deal further than would have been approved of at the end of the century. Once fashionable taste and natural conservatism were lined up together, the likelihood that country houses would be preserved rather than 'restored' became increasingly strong. The story of Combe Abbey in Warwickshire is a case in point. Here a medieval abbey had been added to and adapted to convert it to a house in the sixteenth century, and half rebuilt in the late seventeenth century. The resulting mixture was obviously ripe for stylistic rationalization, and around 1860 W. E. Nesfield, on the strength of the few surviving medieval fragments, produced an ambitious design for rebuilding the whole complex in Early English and fifteenth-century styles. Only one wing of this was built and then work stopped, partly, perhaps, for reasons of finance but perhaps as much because of change in fashion. W. Niven in his *Old Warwickshire Houses* of 1878 expresses cautious disapproval of Nesfield: admittedly 'in a house which has thus gradually *grown* there is of course a good deal of irregularity in the plan, and some inconvenience in communication'; but even so, 'although the new work possesses merits of its own, we cannot regret that the work of reconstruction has gone no further'. Thirty-one years later H. Avray Tipping, writing in *Country Life*, pitched into Nesfield much more vigorously, for by then the SPAB point of view was firmly in the ascendency: 'The history of the place, its gradual evolution, its architectural value and sentimental charm, as representing the varying phases of the native Renaissance Spirit, made no appeal to him.' As for the house, it was 'an epitome of English building craft. . . . Time, the drill master, is ever at work to replace odd garments with a complete and harmonious uniform'.[35]

Time, the drill master, remained on the whole the hero of the country house scene, and country houses were allowed to remain as unpurged illustrations of growth. There was, of course, an exception: the growth philosophy was often not strong enough to counteract the violent twentieth-century reaction against all things Victorian. In the case of country houses the reaction was accentuated by the understandable bitterness of owners with shrinking incomes who found themselves landed with houses enlarged by the Victorians to twice the size they could afford. In many houses all traces of the Victorian period were removed, and the belief grew up that the Victorian period was a black one for the country house. The purpose of this article is to suggest that the true story was a more complex one, a mixture of admirable tact, understandable caution, depressing clumsiness and unforgivable purism. Actual destructiveness is rare; but so, for that matter, is the ability to alter creatively. Hungerford Pollen's redecoration of the Long Gallery at Blickling was inevitably stigmatized by *Country Life* in 1930 as a typical example of Victorian 'misplaced zeal'.[36] But whatever else it was, the, to my view, superbly successful vamping up of the Jacobean decoration with violently un-Jacobean stripes and chunky joinery was certainly not typically Victorian; indeed in surveying the period's long record of good intentions not always achieved one could have done with more of this kind of brilliant buccaneering.

*Blickling, Norfolk, the Jacobean Long Gallery redecorated in the 1860s. The ceiling is original*

*The Ball Room, Pension Building, Washington, as it was in the nineteenth century. The building has been preserved after proposals for demolition, and is now used as offices*

# VII Conservation in America: national character as revealed by preservation

THERE ARE many differences between the preservation movements in Britain, the United States, Canada and Australia, for each movement is the product of a unique historical world-view. The ways in which people view their past are to a considerable extent reflected in those objects that they choose to preserve as reminders of themselves, much as individuals retain faded snapshots as symbolic reminders of early triumphs. Awareness of the past no doubt goes deeper in European societies than in the so-called fragment societies, of which the United States is one; yet Americans are rather more obsessed with their history than Britons are, because Americans are constantly appealing to that history as justification for their plans for the future, whereas in Britain, there is relatively little use of history as a future-related weapon. In this sense the United States is older than Britain itself, because the historical preservation movement, like the national parks movement, is a comparatively young movement in the United Kingdom. Americans, self-conscious of their sense of destiny, began to mark the precise spots of their development while their Revolution was still in progress.

One of the most interesting contrasts arises from the dates of the founding of the professional historical associations in the two countries. The American Historical Association dates from the 1880s. The Historical Association, on the other hand – and does not a little arrogance lurk behind that title '*The* Historical Association'? – was not created until 1906. One might conclude from this juxtaposition of dates that Americans have needed to be more aware of the history around them, and that Americans have had to concentrate at an even earlier date than Britain upon the preservation of the environment because of the rapidity of change in the United States. The rapidity of change itself, and efforts to resist that change, have brought about a set of attitudes towards both history and historical preservation which differ from those attitudes found on the Continent, attitudes which are, however, roughly similar to those found in Australia or Canada, so that they may be thought of as attitudes unique to new societies.

'The Future of the Past' is a fascinating title. For Americans there has always been, of course, far more future than there has been past. Because there is so much obsession with the future, the use of the past in the United States always has been turned towards the interests of the future, toward a bias of utility. What does one want the future to be, and who is it that is doing the wanting? In a society such as the United States, there is much worry about the relevance of human and especially past human action. That which we teach, that which we say, those things which we preserve, must be relevant and invariably relevant to some future point. The past must be usable, it must help define future goals for the nation.

One can define future goals both negatively and positively. There are those who clearly want Americans to preserve the symbols of that which others most want to forget. There is a substantial movement in the United States today for the preservation of a variety of Indian war battlefield sites, including those battlefields which reflect the least honour on the US army of the time. To many all that history consists of is the placing of a finger of blame upon someone; for such there is a need to preserve a series of guilt symbols. More traditionally, Americans wish to preserve that which they want to remember, and it is interesting to look at what is revealed about Americans in their choice of that which they want to remember. A nation's pride is marked by that which it preserves. Quite recently I was in Bucharest where one of the grandest buildings is the Museum of the History of the Romanian Communist Party. Since I read no Romanian the hour I spent there was not specific-ally informative, but the tone, the aura, the purpose of the place were clear enough. This museum was an important contribution to the Romanians' image of themselves. Certainly the Museum of the History of the Romanian Communist Party is not unlike similar museums in other countries, albeit with less didactic titles, such as the Museum of Freedom recently opened in the United States, or the revolutionary museums in Paris, Nicosia or Peking. There are a great number of museums in the United States which are dedicated to free enterprise, of course: country stores, trading posts, preserved factories, etc.

But in societies like the United States, which have fought civil wars, which have been sundered ethnically, which have been divided federally, exactly what the 'nationality' consists of is difficult to define. Many of the objects preserved in America speak not to the nation so much as to the pride of a particular group which has been counter-national. Thus, such historical preservation movements are bound to be negative with respect to someone else, because they almost always emphasize disasso-ciation, separation or schism in one form or another. In the United States the most important of the national heroes no doubt has been Abraham Lincoln, the figure by which every American was able to tell whether in fact he felt himself to be authentically American or not, the hero that all those who arrived as immigrants were to subscribe to equally, the kind of figure to whom one could attribute any nineteenth-century witticism on the grounds that if Lincoln did not say it, he would have had it occurred to him to do so. The Greek temple in Washington, dedicated to Lincoln, indicates precisely the role that he came to play in the American mind, just as Americans would evolve a series of extremely complex and often highly sophisticated national symbols – far more so, virtually, than any other country. Can any other nation in the world, in addition to having a national anthem and a national flag, have a national bird, a national motto and a national flower?

Most such historical preservation movements begin locally. Most arise from local historical societies which are bastions of localism. One expects them to be interested in preserving sites of local importance, which they might reason also have national importance. In one small town in America there is a plaque on an old building declaring it to stand where the first drugstore (or pharmacy) had been built in that state. As a child in that small town, this seemed to me a terribly important fact. Looking back on it today, I still think it an important fact, not because it mattered that the first drugstore in one state had been built there, but because the discovery of that plaque made me decide to become an historian. That is to say, the educational or the persuasive function of historical preservation is to me perhaps the most important end result of what begins for many as an aesthetic and filiopietistic function. There is today a plaque in a small town in California that marks the spot where the first petrol pump in America was erected, and there is a plaque upon every house in which any president of the United States has been born.

The placing of an historical plaque, as opposed to the preservation of the historical object itself, is obviously not so satisfactory. The object has five, whereas the plaque has at most three, specific functions: there is the object of pride, there is the object of commemoration – both plaque and place will do these. There is the function of education, and again plaque and place will do this. But there are two other functions that are more practical. There is the function of preservation, and there is the function of promoting an aesthetic environment. These are increasingly seen to be in an unholy alliance between preservation and tourism, as American businessmen discover that the tourist dollar can be attracted to an area only if, in fact, that area is preserved in a way sufficiently attractive to attract the tourist dollar – an obviously circular argument which has, nonetheless, taken some time to be understood even in an ecclesiastical city such as Canterbury, which the City Fathers have unalterably destroyed.

Historical plaques often remind us of hatreds we are not meant to loose. In France, Italy, Austria, Yugoslavia and Poland one is struck with the number of houses to which are affixed plaques stating that a person was killed by the Nazis at that spot. This is rather more a cemetery than a historical preservation movement, and one may wonder about a city such as Krakow in which Goethe once lived, which lacks a plaque to that fact. One can turn to Canada to find that of the 852 historical plaques erected there upon all varieties of buildings, cairns and sites, the over-whelming majority relate in some way to the United Empire loyalists and the founding of Canada – almost never to the French Canadians, except to be sure, in the province of Quebec itself. One of the firmest defenders of the Dominion is the Historical Sites Board of Canada, which reminds those who read plaques as they run just how much Canada has always had to fear from the United States. Further, there are an interesting number of plaques, some historically inaccurate, placed along the border, which relate to events that people feared might happen, rather than events that did happen.

Of course, Americans are the same. Quite recently, the United States government declared the Star Spangled Banner House in Baltimore, Maryland, to be a national historical landmark under the 1966 Registered National Historic Landmarks Act. Nothing occurred in the Star Spangled Banner House, except that a young lady named Pickersgill pieced together a flag which ultimately became The Flag that flew over Fort McHenry in the War of 1812, when Francis Scott Key wrote the words to the national anthem. This site, then, is a contribution to the intellectual and social history of the country. Such sites are not alone reflections of that intellectual history – they are ongoing contributions to it. Now I mean a little more by this than the fact that if we preserve the good building today this will give a generation later an opportunity to appreciate that good building. I mean a little more by it than the notion that some people are unduly influenced by antiquity and wish to preserve only the ancient and not the recent. Preservationists thus influence the image that the future will have of its past, and by inversion, of the image of what the future will be or ought to be. Intellectual history, as historian James Malin has remarked, is like trying to nail jelly to the wall. Those solid plaques on those solid walls of European capitals are paradoxical: they both relate future to past with a singular presence and they tell us of changing views of the intellectual values of the past. They are a public historiography.

But let me be personal and let me be specific. When walking in London I never fail to stop when I see one of those Wedgwood blue affirmations of a relationship between structure and person. From the London Greater Council booklet that lists all of the plaques one learns that in London alone there are plaques to eighty literary figures, and there are plaques to only four figures in law. If I were the historian of the future, would I not conclude that, by twenty times over, London must have contributed more to literature than the law? Obviously this is not the case; rather, the proportion reflects the fact that historical preservationists are themselves bookish people, obviously more inclined to preserve literary than legal sites. Again, there are forty-seven plaques to the visual arts. There are ten plaques to music, there are twenty-three to science, and both seem out of proportion to the other figures.

This brings us back to national character. What do people wish to be remembered by? In what form will remembrance actually express itself? One looks north to the National Trust of Scotland, to find seventeen castles and twelve gardens. One learns that there is not a single industrial site of any kind that has been preserved by that Trust, while four battles have been commemorated in some form. One might think Disraeli right: these choices represent one only of the 'two nations' of class.

In the United States there are forty-nine national parks, an incredible variety of national historic sites, a large number of national historic parks, a number of national memorials and over nine hundred national historic registered landmarks. In all something like a thousand areas and sites have been preserved by the Federal government – not by state governments – and all are symbols of the search for a national identity. The greatest effort in preservation has been put into Revolutionary War and Civil War battlefields. (Compared to this effort, the preservation of the battlefields of England is pitiful indeed. One would not expect the whole of Bosworth Field to have been preserved; the fifteenth century is long ago, land is valuable agriculturally, and Market Bosworth is not a town to which tourists are drawn in any great number. But one would have liked some indication there, other than the weedgrown field that I found recently, of the momentous occasion it represents.) Still, the greatest single number of sites in the United States relate to two wars, in a nation where the people have argued that there is no military tradition. One might have even predicted, by studying the historical preservation movement in America, that a militarism would emerge on the basis of what it was that Americans had chosen to preserve – not because of such preservation but from what it revealed about their sense of pride.

There are other interests, of course. The second highest number of preserved sites relates to the westward movement and the romantic dream of the Frontier. They consist of a variety of log cabins, marked river crossings, Indian battle sites, places where prospectors and miners worked. The third greatest number of sites preserved is those which relate to business and enterprise. Indeed, the Registered National Historic Landmarks Act clearly specified that examples should be chosen of every type of American business enterprise for preservation. Thus there is a steel mill, an iron rolling works, a coal mine, a locomotive factory, preserved as the best examples of their particular form of industry. It is right that they should be preserved; nonetheless, just as the historian looks back upon these sites in the manner of Macaulay's Maori at Westminster Bridge, he might conclude that Americans were preoccupied with the military, with the westward movement and with business. In truth, these have been American preoccupations, and thus the historical preservation movement is a genuine mirror of what Americans think of themselves.

Yet, what does it reveal when the Federal government decides to preserve the college gymnasium at Westminster College in Fulton, Missouri? This gymnasium was where Winston Churchill coined that magnetic phrase 'the Iron Curtain'. The unhappy girls of Westminster College cannot now have an enlarged gymnasium because of the words that happened to be said there, and the Federal government of the United States has decided that, for all time, 'the Iron Curtain' will itself remain a significant historical truth. Or what is one to make of the preservation of the first site from which nuclear-powered flight took place? Quite legitimately, one would assume that Americans were dedicating this site to the future of modern technology. But they have not preserved the White Sands site where the first atomic bomb was exploded, and only one of the laboratories associated with the true scientific breakthroughs. In short, what they have preserved is a site associated with technological rather than theoretical, purely scientific, achievement.

Now we come full circle back to my first and final point: that those who are historical preservationists have three serious biases. One is that they are bookish, and historical preservation movements tend to over-emphasize the literary and artistic forms of human endeavour. Equally important, those who are interested in historical preservation movements are inclined to wish to shape the view of the future in terms of the positive, in terms of the technologically progressive, in terms of that which influences the lives of people in a visible and dramatic way. Theoretical science is not visible. The preservation of Melk, the greatest monastery of Austria, where Gregor Mendel carried out his experiments with his peas, was achieved not because of Mendel's contribution to genetics, but because of the architectural wonders of the monastery itself. For preservationists also have a bias toward the visible, the still standing structure. In America there is a sense of place, of preserving hallowed ground, even though little remains associated with the events that took place there; in Europe, there is a sense of the object. In both, however, the symbols must be visible – the visible symbols of an invisible past.

*Abraham Lincoln's birthplace memorial in Kentucky, with (inside it) the traditional log cabin in which he was born*

*Abraham Lincoln on his deathbed, in the house opposite Ford's Theatre, Washington, to which he had been carried after being shot by John Wilkes Booth, 14 April 1865. The room (below) is now preserved as a national monument*

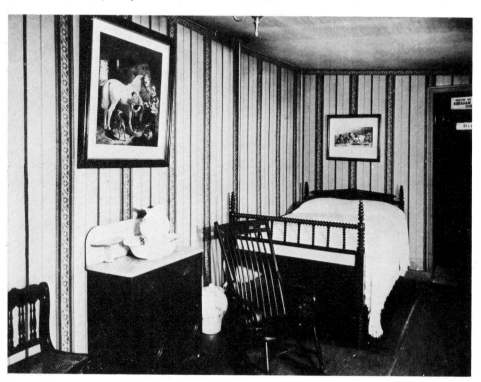

*Sagamore Hill, the home of Theodore Roosevelt*

*The Saugus Iron Works, Massachusetts, preserved as a relic of the Industrial Revolution in America*

# VIII Old sites and new buildings: the architect's point of view

## HUGH CASSON

THIS BOOK is about preservation. It is written by people who look at, use and love architecture but who do not create it. For those of us who do, this difference is crucial. We architects, planners, designers, engineers are builders. Yet we know that more often than not to build is also to destroy. It is as if each time a painter started on a new canvas he was told that the work of another artist would have to be destroyed. How often, one wonders, would his hand be stayed by this news? How, too, would we all react to a system of the spot-listing by anonymous experts of privately and publicly owned art? These questions are luckily academic but are not unfair. They help to explain why some people suspect the sincerity of the architect's love of old buildings, and why some architects believe that the nation is in danger of being stifled by the past.

Is this in fact really what is happening? Or – something more discouraging for architects – is it true that buildings are often being preserved today not so much for their architectural merit as through fear of what will replace them? And if this indeed be so, is it due to greater visual sensitivity or to lack of confidence, to a more sophisticated awareness or just nostalgia masquerading as architectural compassion?

Does it matter, say the preservationists, and can you be surprised? Just take a look around. Buildings speak louder than words, and no amount of protestation from my profession about 'forces beyond our control' or the nature of the acquisitive and apathetic society we serve, can cancel out the faceless banality of what we see around us. Architects, never averse to wearing a hair-shirt, don't mind taking some of the blame for this, but they should not be expected to take all of it. The forces that shape our environment are indeed strong, and seldom helpful. Consider the hysterical rise in land values in outward-moving rings from city centres as the middle-class occupation troops take over and push out the lower-income workers (conservationists often forget the social disruption of their policies); the dark depths of plot ratios, daylight codes, planning control mechanisms in which cruise the entrepreneurs, bright-eyed and slippery; the shadow-boxing of public inquiries and the ceaseless bombardment of traffic (no use listing a conservation area but failing to discipline the motor car); the unpredictability of those price yardsticks and government subsidies that dance like tin-cans on the tails of political whimsy or economic fashion.

No wonder perhaps we cling to what we know, or that, guiltily aware of what first-class building we have allowed to disappear, we place exaggerated value on the second or even fourth-rate.

Excusable this may be. Dangerous it is, for it can lead to paralysis of cultural nerve. A new building is not always to be dreaded, nor is a city or street necessarily the worse for receiving it. We do no good service to the cause of conservation by springing to everything's defence. In this particular battle selectivity is all. The battlefield is boundless and crowded. We have in this country hundreds of towns of all sizes in need of new buildings which, it must be repeated, inevitably mean the loss of old ones. To insert the new into the old requires the highest degree of skill and imagination in every case. (Let nobody subscribe to the view that care has only got to be taken in 'historic' towns and that those less fortunate are not worth worrying about.) Clearly the deep-freeze glass-case solution is unrealistic and cowardly. Equally unalluring are the let-the-people-free-ways of Los Angelism, the tyrannical plug-in megastructures or the do-it-yourself environments so publicized by the modish. The rules are simple, for there are none. Every case is unique, every situation different. Precedent is an unreliable guide, judgment more important than justice, quality than period. Respect for architectural neighbours means more than the meaningless pleasantry. There are occasions for the quick return, the wise-crack, the spirited exchange between individuals.

It is a commonplace to remark that all towns or building groups are more than a sum of their parts. Each is composed of a complex succession of artefacts which have been pieced together over the years into a behavioural pattern that gives use and pleasure to those who live in them. Buildings, in other words, live together like people, with occasional quarrels, mild bickerings, constant compromise, respect for individuals, plus the odd flight of passion or fancy. To search out, analyse and enrich this pattern demands an unusual degree of sophisticated insight and awareness. Gordon Cullen has suggested that there should be a new profession of 'Conceptors', men who can evaluate the nature of the scene and then convert it into a concept within the framework of which new buildings can comfortably (or energetically) sit. Surely, it will be said, this is what happens already in the offices of planning authorities? Here a concept or plan exists, controls are applied, guidance given. True. But save in exceptional circumstances this valuable work on the whole conscientiously carried out by serious-minded persons, can do little more than hold the ring until it disintegrates. Should there then be a law? No. Today's legislation is well-aimed, liberal and firm. (Most recent – and most welcome – is the switch in emphasis from control by intervention to a requirement that the planning authority take positive action instead of sitting around.)

How well then does the machinery work? Unevenly. Conservation areas are proudly designated often only to be mutilated. Specialists are few and lacking in expertise. Proper techniques for the systematic and rapid analysis of data – speed and sequence are as important as ideas – are seldom available. Architects too often lack the relevant insight, operational competence and 'sense of place'. J. M. Richards has suggested that perhaps this trouble might partially be solved if there were more genuinely 'local' architects – men who, like the local GP, acquire a long-term relationship with the neighbourhood in their care. They would know the history of every bump and scar, natural or man-made, what changes are taking place and why, and keep an eye open for the unexpected symptoms. Above all they would live there, calling in specialists and consultants only on special cases and 'doing' – as Dolci says – 'small things well'. Obviously there is merit in this idea, but no amount of tinkering can disguise the fact that we are dealing not so much with professional competence, as with national attitudes and values.

These are sometimes dismissed as being middle-class values. In a sense they are, because only the middle class has the education, leisure, will and cash to fight for them. But in truth they are universal values, and nowhere more universally felt than in the human need for familiarity, stability, for a sense of place. This is what lies behind our unsure society's newly shown hunger for conservation. While architects as members of this society must respect and share this hunger, it is their duty to point out the dangers of over-indulgence, and to warn that if the forces of the market place are to be resisted, other outlets must be found for economic pressures.

Meanwhile the immediate problems remain, and none of them is easy. Should you refuse demolition until satisfied with the quality of the replacement, or should the threatened and the proposed each fight its own battle on its own ground? If a distinguished Victorian architect has inserted his vigorous personal signature into an anonymous Regency terrace, is this gesture – unthinkable (perhaps alas?) today – to be indefinitely preserved? Need period houses necessarily be preserved for ever only for living in? Are the social consequences of preservation sufficiently examined by amenity societies – or can they justifiably say that's somebody else's job? Can progress be justified just by faster traffic flows? Is it inevitable that planning decisions rest only on the value of judgment of a few not necessarily well-informed or sensitive individuals? Are ginger-groups or community forums useful weapons or added confusions? How can the new and welcome public concern be channelled into commitment and action? Only, as always, through the constant effort of individuals, the vigilant and the persistent, the incorrigibly high-spirited and the creative cranks, who alone or as members of groups and societies have built up this great engine of concern and who now must maintain and thoroughly direct its energies.

# Notes on the text

## I  The law's delays

1 Bede, *A History of the English Church and People*, trs. and ed. Leo Sherley-Price, London, 1955.

2 *Of the burning and repair of the church of Canterbury in the year 1174*, from the Latin of Gervase, a monk of the Priory of Christ Church, Canterbury, ed. Charles Cotton, 1930, *Canterbury Papers* No. 3.

3 N. Pevsner, *Buildings of England: London*, I, London, 1962, p. 376.

4 Joan Evans, *A History of the Society of Antiquaries*, Oxford, 1956, p. 1.

5 Joan Evans, *op. cit.*, p. 1.

6 Lucy Toulmin Smith (ed.), *The Itinerary of John Leland*, 1906–10, p. 267.

7 Proclamation against breaking or defacing monuments of antiquity set up in churches, or converting church bells to private use, 19 September 1560, Windsor. Public Records Office, SP. 12/13, 32/33 76.

8 *The most noble antiquity of Great Britain, Vulgarily called Stone-Heng, on Salisbury Plain Restored by Inigo Jones, Esq.; Architect General to the King. Dedicated to the Earl of Pembroke, by John Webb, 1655.*

9 William Dugdale, *History of St Paul's Cathedral*, 1818 ed., 2H.

10 'Superstition & Idolatory, &c.', Journals of the House of Commons, Vol. 2, 1640–42, p. 72, 23–25 January, A.1640, 16. Car. I.

11 Minute Book, Society of Antiquaries of London, from January 1718 to October 1732, Vol. I, p. 46.

12 Minutes of Council of the City of Bristol, 21 July 1733.

13 William Stukeley, Society of Antiquaries Library, MSS. II.

14 Society of Antiquaries, P. 3, Papers (including Papers Read), 1773–80.

15 John Carter, rhyming letter to James Moore, 24 July 1797, Ashmolean Museum, Department of Fine Arts, Moore–Miller papers.

16 Joan Evans, *op. cit.*, p. 207.

17 William Morris, Speech at Annual Meeting of SPAB, Report 1889.

18 John Ruskin, *Seven Lamps of Architecture*, Library edition of *Collected Works*, ed. E. W. Cook and A. Wedderburn, London, 1903–12, Vol. VIII, p. 245, paragraph 20.

19 Proceedings of the Society of Antiquaries, Second Series, Vol. VI, 1875, pp. 29–31.

20 Wayland Kennet, *Preservation*, London, 1972. Chapter I deals, among other historical topics, with the passage of Lubbock's Bill through both Houses.

21 The Ancient Monuments Protection Act (1882), 45 & 46 Vict., Ch. 73.

22 Society of Antiquaries, Correspondence, letter from Rev. J. A. Bennett, 21 March 1889.

23 The National Trust Act (1907), 7 Edw. 7, Ch. 136.

24 The Ancient Monuments Protection Act (1900), 63 & 64 Vict., Ch. 34.

25 The Ancient Monuments Consolidation and Amendment Act (1913), 3 & 4 Geo. 5, Ch. 32.

26 Hermione Hobhouse, *Lost London*, London, 1971, pp. 8, 9, 27. Miss Hobhouse provides 'chapter and verse' on the relevance of the plight of 75 Dean Street to the 1913 Act.

27 Ancient Monuments Consolidation and Amendment Bill (Second Reading), House of Lords, 30 April 1913, Vol. XI, pp. 893–94.

28 The Ancient Monuments Act (1931), 21 & 22 Geo. 5, Ch. 16.

29 The Town and Country Planning Act (1932), 22 & 23 Geo. 5, Ch. 48.

30 The Bath Corporation Act (1937), Edw. 8 and Geo. 6, Ch. 117.

31 Lord Rosse, President's Conference Address, Georgian Group Interim Report, 1969, p. 5.

32 The Town and Country Planning Act (1944), 7 & 8 Geo. 6, Ch. 47.

33 The Town and Country Planning Act (1947), 10 & 11 Geo. 6, Ch. 51.

34 Instructions to Investigators (unpublished), drawn up and circulated in 1946, by S. J. Garton, then Chief Investigator.

35 Evidence submitted to the Committee on Houses of Outstanding Historic or Architectural Interest, HMSO, June 1950.

36 The Historic Buildings and Ancient Monuments Act (1953), 1 & 2 Eliz. 2, Ch. 49.

37 The Local Authorities (Historic Buildings) Act (1962), 10 & 11 Eliz. 2, Ch. 36.

38 Lord Kennet (Wayland Young) 'Achievements and Prospects', *Architectural Review*, Vol. CXLVIII, 886, December 1970, pp. 349–51. Though, here, Lord Kennet is referring to the Civic Amenities Act 1967, and not the 1932 Act.

39 Lord Esher, Annual Report 1959–60, Victorian Society Annual General Meeting, 1 April 1959, p. 4.

40 The Civic Amenities Act (1967), Ch. 69.

41 The Town and Country Amenities Act (1974), Ch. 32.

42 The Town and Country Planning Act (1968), Ch. 72.

43 Pastoral Measure, 16 & 17 Eliz. 2, Vol. II, p. 2427.

## II  Scrape and Anti-scrape

1 *Architectural Review*, CIII, 1948, pp. 91 ff.

2 N. Pevsner, *Buildings of England: Cumberland and Westmoreland*, London, 1967, pl. 42.

3 *Ibid.*, pls. 41 and 43.

4 *Art Bulletin*, XXXVII, 1955, p. 235. Also N. Pevsner, *The Buildings of England: Cambridgeshire*, 2nd ed., London, 1970, p. 28.

5 *The Complete Works of Sir John Vanbrugh*: IV, *The Letters*, ed. G. Webb, London, 1927, p. 29. I have quoted this passage before in my *Outline of European Architecture*, London, 1951, but could hardly avoid the duplication.

6 It was preceded by Carter's *British Topography* in 1780 and followed by the edition of Camden's *Britannia* in 1789. He would deserve a monograph to himself, as would Carter. I have used for Carter's life mainly the entry in the *DNB* by Warwick Wroth, but in addition of course for the whole Wyatt controversy, the *Gentleman's Magazine*; Martin S. Briggs, *Goths and Vandals*, London, 1952; and Joan Evans, *A History of the Society of Antiquaries*, Oxford, 1956.

7 'Grove nods at grove, Each alley has a brother and half the platform just reflects the other' says Pope disapprovingly in landscape terms in his *An Epistle to the Right Honourable Richard Earl of Burlington*, London, 1731.

8 It is the work of John Oldrid Scott.

9 'Diary of Joseph Farington' (BM typescript).

10 *Gentleman's Magazine*, LX, 1790, p. 788.

11 *Ibid.*, LXIII, 1793, p. 125.

12 *Ibid.*, LIX, 1789, p. 874.

13 *Ibid.*, LX, 1790, p. 908.

14 *Ibid.*, LXIII, 1793, p. 178.

15 *Ibid.*, LXV, 1795, p. 785.

16 *Ibid.*, LXV, 1795, p. 924. Viator was answered, and he answered back: *Ibid.*, pp. 998, 1074; LXVI, 1796, pp. 98, 193, 299, 385.

17 Joan Evans, *op. cit.*, p. 207.

18 Rev. J. Milner, 'Dissertation of the modern style of altering antient Cathedrals', p. vi.

19 *Ibid.*, pp. 41 ff.

20 *Ibid.*, p. 19.

21 *Ibid.*, pp. 51 ff.

22 *Gentleman's Magazine*, LXVIII, 1798, p. 476.

23 *Ibid.*, LXIX, 1799, p. 92.

24 *Ibid.*, LXX, 1800, pp. 214–16.

25 *Ibid.*, LXXI, 1801, pp. 413 ff.

26 John Carter, *Specimens of Ancient Sculpture and Painting*, London, 1780–94; *Views of Ancient Buildings in England*, London, 1786–93; *The Ancient Architecture of England*, London, 1795–1814.

27 *Gentleman's Magazine*, LXVIII, 1798, p. 714.

28 *Ibid.*, LXXII, 1802, p. 128.

29 *Ibid.*, LXIX, 1798, p. 27.

30 J. S. Leatherbarrow, London, 1954, p. 74.

31 B. Ferrey, *Recollections of A. C. Pugin and A. W. N. Pugin*, London, 1861; M. Trappes Lomax, *Pugin. A Medieval Victorian*, London, 1932; D. Gwynne, *Lord Shewsbury, Pugin and the Catholic Revival*, London, 1946; S. Gordon Clark, 'A. W. N. Pugin', in *Victorian Architecture*, ed. P. Ferriday, London, 1963. Mrs P. Stanton's excellent *Pugin*, London, 1972, came out, after I had delivered my lecture and transformed it into this paper.

32 J. F. White, *The Cambridge Movement*, Cambridge, 1962, especially pp. 156 ff.

33 B. Ferrey, *op. cit.*, p. 156.

34 A. W. N. Pugin, *The True Principles of Pointed or Christian Architecture*, London, 1841, p. 9.

35 *Ecclesiologist*, I, 1842, p. 70.

36 J. F. White, *op. cit.*, p. 158.

37 *Ecclesiologist*, I, 1842, p. 65.

38 *Ibid.*, IV, 1845, p. 104.

39 *Ibid.*, V, 1846, p. 77.

40 *Ibid.*, VII, 1847, p. 237.

41 *Ibid.*, XXVIII, 1867.

42 'The Church Restorers', *Architectural Review*, CXXXVI, 1964, pp. 87 ff.

43 George Gilbert Scott, reprinted in *Personal and Professional Recollections*, London, 1878, pp. 400 ff.

44 Pishey R. Thompson, *The History and Antiquities of Boston*, Boston, 1856, p. 167.

45 Ferriday, *op. cit.*, p. 92.

46 *Dictionnaire raisonné de l'architecture*, Paris, 1854–58, VIII, the first sentence of the article '*Restauration*'.

47 E. T. Cook and A. Wedderburn, *The Works of John Ruskin*, VIII, London, 1903, pp. 242–44.

48 *Ibid.*, XXXIV, 1903, pp. 513 ff.

49 *Ecclesiologist*, X, 1850, p. 118.

50 Joan Evans, *op. cit.*, p. 309.

51 B. F. L. Clarke, *Church Builders of the Nineteenth Century*, London, 1938, p. 159.

52 P. Henderson, *The Letters of William Morris*, London, 1950, p. 85.

53 *Ibid.*, p. 12.

54 *Ibid.*

55 *Ibid.*, p. 120.

56 Royal Institute of British Architects, *Sessional Papers*, 1876–77, pp. 219 ff.

57 P. Henderson, *op. cit.*, p. 314.

## V  A restoration tragedy

1 Society for Protection of Ancient Buildings, *Annual Report*, 1904, p. 76.

2 J. W. Mackail, *The Life of William Morris*, London, 1899, p. 344.

3 Letter to Richard Gough from Horace Walpole, 1789.

4 Murray, *Cathedrals of England*, Western Division, 1864, p. 70.

5 Anon., *Hereford Cathedral, City and Neighbourhood*, 1867, p. 36.

6 Murray, *op. cit.*, pp. 63, 80–81.
7 B. Ferrey, *Recollections of A. Welby Pugin*, London, 1861, pp. 80–81.
8 *Ibid.*, p. 85.
9 Joan Evans, *A History of the Society of Antiquaries*, Oxford, 1956, p. 212.
10 J. W. Mackail, *op. cit.*, p. 277.
11 E. W. Brayley, *The History and Antiquities of the Abbey Church of St Peter, Westminster*, London, 1818, Vol. 1, pp. 26–27.
12 Murray, *op. cit.*, p. 70.
13 *Statement of the Lord Lieutenant of the County*, February 1864, on the progress of restoration. Worcester Cathedral Archives.
14 *Builder*, 1857, p. 559.
15 G. G. Scott, *Personal and Professional Recollections*, London, 1879, p. 357.
16 G. G. Scott, 'On the Present Position and Future Prospects of the Revival of Gothic Architecture' in *Associated Architectural Societies' Reports and Papers*, Vol. IV, 1857, p. 80.
17 G. G. Scott, *op. cit.*, p. 280.
18 *Builder*, 1875, p. 571.
19 *An Account of the Progress* (of the restoration), 6 August 1851. Bodleian Library, Oxford.
20 James Bentham, *The History and Antiquities of the Conventual and Cathedral Church of Ely*, 2nd ed., Norwich, 1812, p. 284.
21 G. G. Scott, *op. cit.*, p. 183.
22 Murray, *Cathedrals of England*, Eastern Division, 1862, p. 183.
23 G. G. Scott, *op. cit.*
24 Murray, *op. cit.*, p. 185.
25 *An Account of the Progress* (of the restoration), 6 August 1851. Bodleian Library, Oxford.
26 George Gilbert Scott, *Restoration of St Alban's Abbey* (Report), 1871. St Alban's Abbey Archives.
27 John Chapple, 'The Restoration of the Abbey of St Albans'. Paper read at meeting of St Albans Architectural and Archaeological Society, 1874.
28 James Thorne, *Handbook to the Environs of London*, London, 1870, p. 532.
29 G. G. Scott, *op. cit.*, p. 200.
30 G. G. Scott, *Gleanings from Westminster Abbey*, Oxford and London, 1861, pp. 31–34.
31 W. R. Lethaby, *Westminster Abbey Re-examined*, London, 1925, p. 102.
32 Letter to the Dean and Chapter of Rochester Cathedral from G. G. Scott. Rochester Cathedral Archives.
33 *Ibid.*
34 *Ibid.*
35 G. G. Scott, *Gleanings from Westminster Abbey*, 1861, pp. 28–29.
36 *Ibid.*
37 SPAB *Annual Report*, 1884, pp. 32–33.
38 G. G. Scott, *Gleanings from Westminster Abbey*, 1861, p. 55.
39 *Ibid.*, pp. 101–2.
40 'Our Future Architecture', *Builder*, 1867, p. 386.
41 Rev. G. L. Prestige, *St Paul's in its Glory*, London, 1955, p. 145.
42 Murray, *Cathedrals of England*, Eastern Division, 1862, p. 77.
43 W. R. Lethaby, 'Westminster Abbey and Its Restoration' in SPAB *Annual Report*, 1902, pp. 71–72.
44 SPAB *Annual Report*, 1902, p, 72.
45 Murray, *Cathedrals of England*, Eastern Division, 1862, p. 118.
46 *Gentleman's Magazine*, April 1847, p. 404.
47 A paper read at the Anniversary Meeting of the Ecclesiological Society, *Ecclesiologist*, XIX, 1858, p. 240.
48 *Ibid.*
49 *Ecclesiologist*, XX, 1859, p. 330.
50 *Ibid.*, p. 217.
51 *Gentleman's Magazine*, January 1792, p. 84.
52 Letter from C. Hodgson Fowler, 26 October 1898. Rochester Cathedral Archives. Emf. 70/1.
53 SPAB *Annual Report*, 1892, p. 40.
54 *Ibid.*, p. 38.
55 *Peterborough Cathedral Restoration*, a report of the Dean and Chapter and the Restoration Committee, 1884. Peterborough Cathedral Archives.
56 SPAB *Annual Report*, 1884, pp. 22–23.

57 Peter Ferriday, *Lord Grimthorpe*, 1957, p. 147.
58 *Ibid.*, p. 147.
59 *Ibid.*, pp. 142–44.
60 *Builder*, 22 September 1888, p. 205.
61 *Ibid.*
62 *Ibid.*
63 SPAB *Annual Report*, 1884, p. 9.
64 G. F. Bodley, 'On some principles and characteristics of ancient architecture', in RIBA *Journal*, Vol. VII, 1899–1900, p. 140.
65 *Ibid.*
66 R. Norman Shaw, Letter to J. D. Sedding, 20 November 1882.
67 SPAB *Annual Report*, 1897, pp. 20–21.
68 SPAB *Annual Report*, 1898, pp. 10–11.
69 A. J. B. Beresford-Hope, *The Art-Workman's Position*, a lecture, 1864.
70 J. W. Mackail, *op. cit.*, p. 202.
71 G. G. Scott, 'On the Present Position and Future Prospects of the Revival of Gothic Architecture' in *Associated Architectural Societies' Reports and Papers*, Vol. IV, 1857, p. 77.
72 *Ibid.*
73 John Ruskin, *The Seven Lamps of Architecture*, London, 1849, p. 210.
74 SPAB *Annual Report*, 1879, p. 34.
75 *Appeal for the restoration of the west front of Lichfield Cathedral*, 1879, Lichfield Cathedral Archives.
76 *Lichfield Diocesan Church Calendar*, 1885.
77 *Builder*, 1876, p. 347.
78 SPAB *Annual Report*, 1897, pp. 29–30.
79 J. H. J. Fletcher, *The Story of Salisbury Cathedral*, 1933, p. 195.
80 Robert Billings, *Architectural Illustrations and Description of the Cathedral Church of Durham*, London, 1843.
81 SPAB *Annual Report*, 1890, pp. 41–42.
82 SPAB *Annual Report*, 1891, p. 35.
83 Murray, *Cathedrals of England*, Eastern Division, 1862, p. 76.
84 Shaw, *Victoria County History: Staffordshire*, p. 260.
85 Lichfield Cathedral Archives, ix 25 v 26.
86 *Gentleman's Magazine*, 1795, p. 924.
87 Lichfield Diocesan Archives, 1862, p. 39.
88 Friends of Salisbury Cathedral Report, 1961.
89 Murray, *Cathedrals of England*, Western Division, 1864, p. 151.
90 Horace Walpole in letter to the Hon. H. S. Conway, 5 August 1789. (From Martin S. Briggs, *Goths and Vandals*, London, 1952, p. 126.)
91 *Builder*, 1877, p. 392.
92 *Ibid.*, 8 January 1876.
93 Georgiana Burne-Jones, *Memorials of Edward Burne-Jones*, Vol. I, 1904, pp. 113–14.
94 From a letter from William Morris to Andreas Scheu, an Austrian refugee and fellow-Socialist, 5 September 1883.
95 From a lecture given by Morris in 1878, 'The Lesser Arts'.
96 H. Wilson, 'Art and Religion', *Architectural Review*, VI, 1899, p. 278.
97 C. R. Ashbee, *Where the Great City Stands. A study in the new civics*, London, 1917, pp. 12–13.
98 *The Times*, 15 August 1890.
99 Joan Evans, *A History of the Society of Antiquaries*, Oxford, 1956, p. 212.
100 *The Athenaeum*, 10 March 1877, and Peter Ferriday, *Lord Grimthorpe*, 1957, p. 109.
101 Joan Evans, *op. cit.*, p. 308.
102 *Ibid.*, p. 309.
103 SPAB *Annual Report*, 1879, p. 27.
104 *Ibid.*, p. 39.
105 *Ibid.*, p. 36.
106 Joan Evans, *op. cit.*, pp. 334–36.
107 SPAB *Annual Report*, 1893.

## VI Living with the past

1 *Country Life*, LXXVII, 18 and 25 May 1940, pp. 502–7, 524–28.
2 M. Girouard, *The Victorian Country House*, London, 1971, pp. 24–26. The introduction discusses the planning requirements of a country house in some detail.
3 *Country Life*, LXXIV, 19 August 1933,

pp. 172–77. The name of the Victorian architect is not known.

4 *Historic Houses of the United Kingdom,* London, 1892, p. 135.

5 The date and architect of these wings haven't been established, though their stylistic reticence suggests the hand of William Burn.

6 *Country Life,* LXV, 16 February 1929, pp. 216–23.

7 For Encombe see *Country Life,* 24 and 31 January 1963, pp. 164–68, 214–17; for Petworth, *ibid.,* 28 November 1925, pp. 818–26; for Longford, *ibid.,* 12, 19 and 26 December 1931, pp. 648–55, 696–702, 724–30.

8 *Ibid.,* LIII, 17 April 1925, pp. 466–73.

9 *Ibid.,* XLII, 3 November 1917, pp. 420–25.

10 *Ibid.,* CXXV, 12 February 1959, pp. 304–7.

11 *Ibid.,* CXXIII, 16, 23 and 30 January 1958, pp. 108–11, 156–59, 202–5.

12 Illustrated, F. O. Morris, *The Country Seats of the Noblemen and Gentlemen of Great Britain and Ireland,* London, 1866–80.

13 *Country Life,* CXLIII, 15 February 1968, pp. 340–44.

14 Information from George Clive.

15 Vulliamy to Holford, 20 September 1866. Westonbirt papers (uncatalogued), RIBA.

16 Alfred Barry, *The Life and Work of Sir Charles Barry,* London, 1867, p. 110; M. Girouard, *op. cit.,* pp. 68–70.

17 *Country Life,* CXXV, 16, 23 and 30 April 1959, pp. 828–31, 890–93, 948–51; M. Girouard, *op. cit.,* pp. 71–72.

18 The 'List of Architectural Designs' in Alfred Barry's *Life* mentions unexecuted designs for Drumlanrig made in 1840. But the detail of the design illustrated (RIBA), from the collection of Barry's great-grandson, C. A. R. Barry (d. 1953), suggests a later date.

19 G. G. Scott, *Secular and Domestic Architecture,* London, 1857, p. 147.

20 A. W. N. Pugin, *The True Principles of Pointed or Christian Architecture,* London, 1841, p. 55.

21 Augustus J. C. Hare, *Story of My Life,* London, 1896–1900, IV, p. 281.

22 E. Salvin's work at Petworth, Burn's 1855 stables at Kinmel and Devey's octagon pavilion at Coombe Warren.

23 It appears as 'Cheverel Manor' in 'Mr Gilfil's Love-Story'. The house is described in Chapter II. The front is admitted to have 'too formal symmetry', but the dining room, 'impressed one with its architectural beauty like a cathedral'.

24 *Country Life,* CXLIX, 13 and 20 May 1971, pp. 1152–56, 1216–19.

25 *Passages from the Diaries of Mrs Lybbe Powys,* ed. E. J. Climenson, London, 1899, p. 387.

26 *Country Life,* CXI, 11 and 18 April, 2 May 1952, pp. 1080–85, 1163–67, 1328–31.

27 *Country Life,* XXXII, 27 July 1912, pp. 126–33; LV, 24 May 1924, pp. 812–19. Brandon's bay and oriel windows were of completely different design to the original ones, and all windows were filled with plate glass; the house was more sensitively 're-restored' by Herbert Baker in the 1920s.

28 Augustus J. C. Hare, *The Story of Two Noble Lives,* London, 1893, I, p. 251.

29 *Ibid., Story of My Life,* III, p. 10; *Country Life,* LXXXIX, 11 January 1941, pp. 32–35.

30 W. R. Lethaby, *Philip Webb and His Work,* London, 1935, p. 111.

31 *Country Life,* CLI, 9 and 16 March, 27 April, 4 May 1972.

32 *Ibid.,* XLI, 7 and 14 April 1917, pp. 352–58, 376–81.

33 *Ibid.,* XXII, 21 September 1907 *et al.,* pp. 414–22.

34 *Ibid.,* CXXXVII, 4, 11 and 18 February 1965, pp. 232–35, 286–89, 352–56.

35 *Ibid.,* XXVI, 4 and 11 December 1909, pp. 794, 844.

36 *Ibid.,* LXVII, 21 June 1930, pp. 902–8.

# Index

Page numbers in italic
indicate illustrations